Defining the Good School

Defining the Good School

Educational Adequacy Requires More Than Minimums

Jeff Swensson and Michael Shaffer

ROWMAN & LITTLEFIELD
Lanham • Boulder • New York • London

Published by Rowman & Littlefield
An imprint of The Rowman & Littlefield Publishing Group, Inc.
4501 Forbes Boulevard, Suite 200, Lanham, Maryland 20706
www.rowman.com

6 Tinworth Street, London SE11 5AL, United Kingdom

Copyright © 2020 by Jeff Swensson and Michael Shaffer

All rights reserved. No part of this book may be reproduced in any form or by any electronic or mechanical means, including information storage and retrieval systems, without written permission from the publisher, except by a reviewer who may quote passages in a review.

British Library Cataloguing in Publication Information Available

Library of Congress Cataloging-in-Publication Data

Names: Swensson, Jeff, author. | Shaffer, Michael (Michael Byran) author.
Title: Defining the good school : educational adequacy requires more than minimums / Jeff Swensson and Michael Shaffer.
Description: Lanham, Maryland : Rowman & Littlefield Publishing Group, 2020. | Includes bibliographical references and index. | Summary: "Mired in an archaic purpose, American schools are inhibited by policies tethered to high minimum quality, the nation's definition of educational adequacy. This book deconstructs the barriers that obstruct the future: contemporary public education. This search uncovers the necessities for transforming educational adequacy for all US students"-- Provided by publisher.
Identifiers: LCCN 2019049619 (print) | LCCN 2019049620 (ebook) | ISBN 9781475856200 (cloth) | ISBN 9781475856217 (paperback) | ISBN 9781475856224 (epub)
Subjects: LCSH: Education--Aims and objectives--United States. | Education--Standards--United States. | Educational change--United States.
Classification: LCC LA217.2 .S923 2020 (print) | LCC LA217.2 (ebook) | DDC 370.11--dc23
LC record available at https://lccn.loc.gov/2019049619
LC ebook record available at https://lccn.loc.gov/2019049620

Contents

Preface		ix
Introduction		xiii
1	**What's the Purpose of Public Education?**	1
	The Contemporary Purpose of Education	1
	The More US Education Changes, the More It Stays the Same	2
	A Selfie Puts Education's Purpose and Educational Adequacy to the Test	3
	What Do We Have Here? Implications from the Selfie	9
	A Future for US Public Education	10
	Beginning to Search with the End in Mind	11
2	**True North: The Moral Obligation of Public Education**	13
	True North and Socialization	13
	Socialization and Moral Obligation in Public Education	14
	The Troubled History of Moral Obligation	15
	Moral Obligation and the Absence of Critical Habits of Mind	17
	The Capacity for Moral Obligation in Public Education	18
	Interpretations of Moral Obligation	20
	Students and Self-Mastery and Principled Reasoning	21
	Choices and the Future of Moral Obligation	22
	Standing in the Way of Moral Obligation	23
	Precepts of the Moral Obligation of US Public Education	24
3	**The Eye of the Beholder: An Unavoidable Barrier**	27
	This Search and Its Barriers	27
	The Perspectives and Publics of Contemporary US Public Education	28
	Major Perspectives about US Public Education	29
	Two Publics in US Public Education	35
	Barriers Arise Where None Should Exist	36
	Taking This Search beyond the Eye of the Beholder	38
4	**A Barrier Within: The Tyranny of Either/Or**	39
	The Synergy of Struggle	39
	The TEO Barrier: School Attached or School Detached	43
	Dismantling the Tyranny of Either/Or	44
5	**Confronting the Barrier of Conventional Wisdom**	47
	The Authority of Conventional Wisdom	47

	The Baleful State of Educational Adequacy	48
	How Educational Adequacy Becomes Conventional Wisdom	50
	Educational Adequacy: A Dead End	51
	Reconsidering Educational Adequacy	52
6	The Measurement Barrier in US Public Education	55
	I-P-O and Measurement: Standardized Testing	55
	Measurement and Its Misnomers	56
	The Fog of Certainty	60
	Measurement and the Illusion Called Gap-Gazing	61
	The Case for Effective Evaluation	63
	The End of Measurement Inadequacy	65
7	Power and Public Education	67
	The Presence of Power in Education	67
	The Rationale for the Future of US Public Education	68
	Power: Abuse and Potential of a Steady State	70
	The Minor Leagues: Purpose, Power, and Education	71
	Why the Original Power of Education Is Vulnerable	72
	The "What," "Who," and "Why" of Power in Education	73
	Power and "I Identify as . . ." Statements	76
	Avoiding the Absolutes: Power + Corruption	77
	Freedom: The Original Power of Education	78
8	Dynamic Instruction: Act I—Function, Evaluation, Precursors	81
	Setting the Stage for Dynamic Instruction	82
	Dynamic Instruction	83
	Act I: Exeunt All	88
9	Dynamic Instruction: Act II—Student Engagement	89
	Student Engagement and Satisfactory Quality	89
	Pedagogical Agency	91
	Languaging and Student Engagement	92
	The Reviews Are In: Dynamic Instruction	95
10	Policy and Idiocy in US Public Education	97
	The Idiocy of Contemporary Educational Policy	98
	The Wreck of the Good Ship Educational Policy	101
	Locally Sourced Policy	102
	Removing Idiocy from the Policy Menu	103
	Common Ground: Policy for the Good Public School	107
11	Recovering the "public" of US Education	109
	The Shared Circumstance of "public" in Education	110
	Common Ground: "public"	112
12	Weaving Educational Adequacy and the Good Public School	115
	Transforming Educational Adequacy	115

	Commitments about Comprehensive Public Education	116
	Choices, Weaving, and Philosophy	116
	The Good Public School: Indicators and Objectives	118
13	Implications from This Search for Educational Adequacy	125
	The Second Implication	126
	The Third Implication	126
	The Fourth Implication	127
	The Fifth Implication	128
	The Sixth Implication	129
	Learning from the Implications of This Search	129
14	Student Futures and Comprehensive Public Education	133
	We Have Met the Enemy and He Is Us	133
	The Benchmarks for *21CPE*	136
	Promises Empower *21CPE*	138
	Dealing with the "If" of *21CPE*	140
	Welcome to the Good Public School	141

References	143
Index	151
About the Authors	153

Preface

> The function of education is to teach one to think intensively and to think critically. Intelligence plus character, that is the goal of true education.
>
> —Martin Luther King

US public educators know how to search. America's parents and caregivers also know how to search. And we search for the same thing: satisfactory quality throughout teaching and learning in public education.

Educators search for professional practices that will grow student capabilities and engage student cognition. We search for meaningful ways to validate and care for all students. We search for support from policymakers and politicians. We search for the attributes, characteristics, professional strategies, and research-based capacities that create educational adequacy.

Parents and caregivers search for the good public school. They search for educational adequacy in public schools where their child's capacities grow and where the lived experience of every student is valorized. Tireless efforts by families everywhere illustrate the value of and necessity for educational adequacy, the harbinger of a good public school.

The search for the good public school illustrates the value attached to educational adequacy by those most dedicated to its presence and its impact. But only a few educators realize, and even fewer parents have a clue, that most of their searches are doomed to fail.

A successful search is rare because the contemporary definition of educational adequacy fails to rise above minimums. Locating the good public school, as a result, becomes a search for the proverbial needle in a haystack.

The first minimum standing in the way of the good public school is the contemporary purpose of US public education. The purpose of US public schools is to prepare students to "fit" the needs of business and industry. The second minimum is the anemic and disconnected definition of educational adequacy that orients public education in America.

Stymied by the dilemmas inherent within the minimums of purpose and adequacy, traditional public education in America also is called upon to fix the ills of society. Handcuffed by purpose and inadequacy while overwhelmed by a tsunami of misaligned demands, US public schools are at a point where power, policy, and practice reinforce inadequacy.

Instead of a clear focus on critical habits of mind, teaching and learning are forced into the narrow confines dictated by standardized achievement tests, ideological mandates, and fiscal restraints.

The good public school should not be discovered on a hit-or-miss basis. Educational adequacy cannot exist when the original power of education is restricted. Under these conditions, educators and parents/caregivers seek the good public school and educational adequacy with the same success that early explorers sought the Northwest Passage.

This book, then, is a search for educational adequacy in the good public school that all students deserve during the remainder of the twenty-first century. Because public schools "exist to achieve public purposes" (Reimers, 2006, p. 275), inadequacy and the contemporary purpose of US education must be transformed.

To be successful, the search for educational adequacy in the good public school must focus on the capabilities and capacities at the core of the original power of education and in the lived experience of all students that facilitate engagement of "the disciplined mind . . . the synthetic mind, the creative mind, the respectful mind and the ethical mind (Gardner, 1993)" (Reimers, 2006, p. 278). Such a pursuit, the breadth of the search undertaken throughout this book, is a search for responses to three questions:

- What is the primary purpose of public education?
- Where are educational adequacy and moral obligation?
- How should professional practice be oriented to engage with a primary purpose, upgrade educational adequacy, fulfill moral obligation, and foster dynamic instruction required for this level of engagement?

The need to deal with these questions is prompted by the extent to which contemporary thinking about a good school is entangled in perpetuation of the inadequacy within conventional wisdom. The need to conduct this search is anchored in an abiding concern that battles between the major perspectives about American schooling divide and disrupt the satisfactory quality required in a good public school.

As this search unfolds, our intent is to locate common ground from which colleagues in US public education can pursue the intersection of the primary purpose and moral obligation that deliver the universality of US public education. Nothing less than a good public school where a transformed understanding of educational adequacy is omnipresent can suffice for the futures that all US students deserve.

American public education began with promises of free and universal. Realization of the full potential of US students lies in the fulfillment of these, and other, promises that lie dormant in contemporary US education. This book is a search for educational adequacy and the good public school on behalf of all US students and on behalf of the democracy that depends on them.

Jeff Swensson
Michael Shaffer
Spring 2020

Introduction

Too many barriers stand in the way of educational adequacy for the good public school in America. This search for educational adequacy, as a result, is undertaken with the intent to surmount these obstacles and to identify the characteristics of what will be referred to as twenty-first-century comprehensive public education (*21CPE*).

We conduct this search, overcome barriers, share insights about a US public education that delivers educational adequacy to all students, and weave a tapestry of the good public school. Our objective is to encourage continuing inquiry and improvement to sustain and grow the good public school. This search entails an examination of the original power of education, the primary purpose of education, and the moral obligation of public education as the responsibilities all traditional public educators must fulfill to ensure that the capacities of all US students are brought to the fore in classrooms throughout our nation.

This search begins with a discussion about the contemporary purpose of public education and about how educational adequacy is understood as the third decade of this century dawns. Purpose and adequacy in US education are stymied, however, by several barriers, and these are confronted in chapters 3 through 6. Our discussion deconstructs these barriers. Clues to the nature of the good public school are considered.

Working past these barriers allows this discussion to explore the determinants of comprehensive public education. In chapters 7 through 11, a discussion of power, dynamic instruction, policy, and "public" gives educators and policymakers benchmarks from scholarship and practice that frame the transformation of educational adequacy and establish the foundation from which the good public school should be initiated.

The future of US public education emerges from this search in chapters 12, 13, and 14. A picture of comprehensive public education, the implications of this search, and the transformation of educational adequacy necessary and sufficient to establish the persistent discovery of the good public school bring this discussion to an end.

The good public school eludes too many parents/caregivers and too many communities. Satisfactory quality, educational adequacy, is missing from the daily learning experiences of too many US students. This book is written because the good public school that all US students deserve for the remainder of the twenty-first century should be the rule and not the exception.

ONE
What's the Purpose of Public Education?

"Now, that's a good school!" Parents and caregivers across the United States frequently identify their local public school with this statement (PDK, n.d.). Caring teachers, a community-wide reputation, good programs, the opinion of other parents, high test scores—all are among the reasons that make a local public school a good school.

At the local level, satisfactory quality and purpose come together in public education when parents and caregivers perceive that their child is happy and making progress. Proclaiming a "good school" means that parents/caregivers believe the school delivers satisfactory quality and fulfills a valuable purpose. Quality and purpose are fulfilled by the tenor of day-to-day learning experiences. Parents and caregivers focus on how a school affects their child.

Considered more broadly, however, attention to the purpose and the adequacy of US public education is less focused. Observers identify satisfactory quality in terms of external factors including available resources, high achievement scores, school or neighborhood affluence, or teacher attitudes (Anyon, 2005). But the extent to which any individual school delivers these or more complex indicators of satisfactory quality or adequacy is too often left to chance.

THE CONTEMPORARY PURPOSE OF EDUCATION

This roll of the educational dice is an enduring characteristic of US public education because the contemporary purpose of teaching and learning is a substantial, if unacknowledged, impediment to the future of all students. Unchanged since the advent of the first public schools in the early

1800s, the purpose of public education is to prepare students for employment.

For more than a century, the purpose of US public education has been galvanized to the fact that "an agricultural and then heavy industrial economy made physical strength the key requirement for work force participation" (Comer, 2015, p. 225). Attention to community values, work habits, respect for authority, the rudiments of knowledge, and a modicum of cognitive process provide backup for "the regular suggestion that students are in school primarily to acquire marketable skills to be cashed in for employment" (Strike, 2008, p. 121).

Under these circumstances, an academically bland school experience has been sufficient to meet the employment needs of most US students. Subject area learning kept pace with the time-honored purpose of American schooling; transitioning over time from reading, writing, and arithmetic to "new" versions of these same subject areas. In the long run, how a good contemporary public school is perceived is based on specious criteria: the eye of the beholder and service to the status quo.

At a Loss to Glimpse the Future

This search for the good public school is necessary because blurry, dim visions of purpose and adequacy leave contemporary public education unable to serve all US students. Contemporary US public education "fuels school practice without attention to purpose" (Reimers, 2006, p. 285). The good public school for all students during the remainder of the twenty-first century eludes the United States because contemporary public education is anchored to a purpose that promotes educational inadequacy.

The goal of this chapter is to examine the failure of US public education to disengage from a purpose that cannot serve all students and their futures. This purpose ensures that adequacy—satisfactory quality—is not a part of the school experiences of too many US students. This state of affairs illuminates the need for a thorough search for educational adequacy that gives all students learning experiences in the good public school.

THE MORE US EDUCATION CHANGES, THE MORE IT STAYS THE SAME

Although employment that necessitates physical strength—among other archaic employment skills—is a vestige of a bygone America, the presumption endures into the current century that the purpose of public education is to develop meaningful economic futures for individuals and the nation (Pritchett and Viarengo, 2015).

With the dawn of the 2000s, for example, participants in the annual conference convened by the Federal Reserve Bank of Boston put their money on conventional wisdom and "agreed that education is increasingly important in determining individuals' earnings potential" (Kodrzycki, 2002, p. 4). Twenty-first-century observers even go so far as to identify an *education industry* (Eng, 2013), whose purpose is to "be able to develop students whose skills match employers' demands" (p. 273).

Public education and its purpose are galvanized to the assumption that employee skills of the present are employee skills of the future. This assumption traps teaching and learning in the deficiencies of the past, the stasis of the present, and an inadequate future throughout US public education. This cul-de-sac of purpose and adequacy leads to "a deficit view of public schools [and] to flawed assumptions, mis-specified problems, and ineffective solutions (Forsyth, Adams, and Hoy, 2011)" (Adams, Ware, Miskell, and Forsyth, 2016, p. 169).

Underlying this point of view is a belief system that undercuts a more profound purpose for public education while it installs survival of the fittest as the singularity that defines life. Advocates of reform in American public schools, for instance, phrase this belief starkly: "If you fail to achieve that good life it is your fault" (Brown, 2002, p. 100). Other critics of US public education double down on this and suggest that "policymakers should expand niche secondary education services to meet employer demand" (Eng, 2013, p. 280).

Deficit views of US public education do not recognize the impact of unsatisfactory quality on student success. Deficit views of US public education suggest that the purpose of school is to restrict the capacities of each student to fit a slot in the job market.

Anchoring public education to a purpose disconnected from the twenty-first century, and anchoring the futures of all students to teaching and learning inadequate to the dynamic between individual freedom and the public good, is a cycle that's difficult to escape. Moreover, anachronisms allied with these deficiencies foster educational stasis and enable leaders to turn a blind eye to the inequities strewn throughout the history of US education.

A SELFIE PUTS EDUCATION'S PURPOSE AND EDUCATIONAL ADEQUACY TO THE TEST

No one picture, no one point of view, no one sketch can do justice to the complexity or potential of US public education. Teaching and learning—at their best—recognize and nurture the innate capabilities that all students bring to the classroom: natural thinking and meaning-making (Ignelzi, 2000). These cognitive behaviors—nurtured by lived experience, culture, race, language, and ethnicity—are among the assets and resources that students apply during their encounters with the world as they learn and grow.

Innate capabilities such as these are the tip of the proverbial cognitive iceberg and signal that individuals have extensive untapped potential in analytical, creative, and practical intelligences (Sternberg, 1997). Policymakers, pundits, politicians, educators, and citizens who are enamored with the contemporary purpose of public education or who believe that public education should be demolished fail to perceive the endless capabilities of all students and fail to advocate for a primary purpose for US public education that *leads-out** student cognition to robust capabilities that serve the individual and society.

[*Authors' Note*: The term *education* is derived from the Latin *educere*, "to lead out." When the professional practices of public educators lead-out, they access students' lived experience and meaning-making to engage with *habits of mind* or thinking skills.]

A brief data selfie contains cues and clues that suggest the imperative for a search for educational adequacy and the good public school. This selfie suggests the need for transforming adequacy and purpose in public education. Elements of the future of public education and a transformed primary purpose that leads-out lie within this snapshot. This snapshot substantiates the need to search for educational adequacy in the good public school for all US students.

A Selfie Reveals . . .

- Near the end of the second decade of the twenty-first century, more than fifty-six million students are enrolled in America's traditional public schools (USDOE, 2018).
- A significant proportion of US teachers are White (82 percent) and female (76 percent) (Minkos et al., 2017, p. 2).
- "Prospective teachers must increasingly teach in schools where they must successfully cross lines of color and class and where many schools have two or more substantial non-White groups and concentrated poverty" (Orfield and Frankenberg, 2014, p. 731).
- As the third decade of the twenty-first century approached, more than three million students are enrolled in America's public charter schools (David and Hesla, 2018).
- At the same time, more than 5.5 million students are enrolled in US private schools and 78 percent of private schools in the United States are religiously affiliated (CAPE, 2018).

[*Authors' Comment:* Too often, numbers of students enrolled are ballyhooed as if they indicate educational adequacy or reform. Our experiences as K–16 educators and our insights into research tell us that if this is quality then this assertion mirrors the erroneous thought process that equates numbers of sandwiches sold at a fast food restaurant with quality cuisine. Our perspective is that instead of aggregations of numbers, the lived experience of students, a primary purpose of public education, and a clear definition of educational adequacy must form the baseline for US public education during the remainder of this century.]

State Authority for Public Education

- "The states must be viewed as 50 separate countries when assessing the status of public education" (Brown, 2002, p. 99).

[*Authors' Comment:* Each state (guided by its constitution) determines the nature of public schools. Aiding and abetting a state's statutory oversight of its educational fiefdom are the federal government and a host of non-governmental actors. The federal government influences selected aspects of schooling across the nation with oversight in areas including civil rights, special education, and reform. Equally profound is the influence of a host of national networks, foundations, and corporations dedicated to advancing free market theory in schools across the United States. The actions of state legislators are influenced profoundly when the dollars, politics, and ideology of free market proponents and federal authorities make and mandate assumptions about purpose and adequacy in public education.]

A Diverse Student Population

- As of 2014, so-called minority students in the United States became the majority of students in traditional public schools and, in 2018, this majority (almost 55 percent) included several cohorts of America's children and young people: Black, Hispanic, Asian/Pacific Islander, American Indian/Alaska Native, and students of two or more races (Chen, 2018).
- "The 43 years from 1968 to 2011 brought a 28% decline in White enrollment, a 19% increase in the Black enrollment, and a 495% increase in the number of Latino students" (Orfield and Frankenberg, 2014, p. 720).
- Data from the USDOE (United States Department of Education) indicates that as of 2016, 19 percent of children under the age of eighteen were in families living in poverty (IES/NCES, 2018).
- Thirty-four percent of Black children and the same percentage of American Indian/Alaska Native children lived in poverty in 2016 while 28 percent of Hispanic children lived in poverty (IES/NCES, 2018).

[*Authors' Comment:* Students of color and students in poverty often are subject to the worst of American education. The euphemism often used to describe this inadequacy is that these students are "underserved." The responsibility for eradicating this persistent state of affairs in education ought to lie with decision makers including state legislators, schools of education, and national leaders. We lament the counterproductive efforts (some unintentional but many deliberate) of these actors and we agree with several scholars that waiting around for appropriate and effective action is not a viable strategy (Smith and Lowery, 2017). As we will illustrate, school districts, schools, and school personnel have the power and the obligation to act on behalf of all students where a host of policymakers and leaders have failed.]

High School Graduation

- The average rate of US high school students graduating from public school within four years of matriculating in the ninth grade (referred to as the Adjusted Cohort Graduation Rate or ACGR) is 84 percent as of the 2015–2016 school year (IES/NCES, 2018).
- The ACGR in the United States for Hispanic students is 79 percent while for Black students the ACGR is 76 percent (IES/NCES, 2018).
- On a state-by-state basis, there is a gap between the Adjusted Cohort Graduation Rate for different racial cohorts. For instance, the gap between the ACGR for White and Black students in Ohio is 20 percentage points. In New York, this same gap is 21, in the District of Columbia it's 23, while in Wisconsin the ACGR gap is 29 (IES/NCES, 2018).

[*Authors' Comment:* This data indicates the abandonment of the intersection between how to think and the moral obligation of public education. Articulating then pursuing a primary purpose in public education on behalf of all students is critical if a focus on this moral obligation is to be restored. Educational adequacy for all US students in public schools entails fulfillment of a moral obligation that cannot be separated from pursuit of a primary purpose. Obligation, adequacy, and purpose in public education must be enriched by the capacities and lived experience of all students.]

Funding for US Education

Financial support for traditional public education in the middle of the second decade of the twenty-first century can be analyzed using different data points:

- On average, 8 percent of a school's budget is provided by federal dollars.
- Forty-seven percent of a school's budget is comprised of state dollars.
- The remaining 45 percent of a school's budget is supplied by local tax dollars (NCES, 2018).

- The total dollars allocated from all three sources to traditional public schools in the United States is approximately $664 billion (NCES, 2018).
- Funding for charter schools, vouchers, and other privatization mechanisms is difficult to quantify because the total is a combination of state tax dollars, tax avoidance contributions, and donations from private sources.

[*Authors' Comment*: Dollars and cents for education are a volatile issue. Critics of traditional public education often contend that too much is spent on education with little of value to show for the expenditures. Free market theory proponents believe that these costs can be reduced significantly when mechanisms like charter schools and vouchers become education and offer efficiencies. Driven by allegiances to efficiencies within adult-centric priorities (e.g., less government, the efficiencies of free market theory, instructional panaceas, or "we've always done things this way"), adequacy of public education devolves into underservice. Sufficient and necessary funding falls victim to the attention paid to political, policy, and other adult imperatives with the result that multitudes of students across the United States pay the price.]

Parents and Caregivers

- Early in the second decade of the twenty-first century, approximately 30 percent of US households included school-age children (Ely and Teske, 2015, p. 176).
- A study analyzing data from 24,867 Black and White students from 101 secondary schools across ten states found 75 percent of White students and 34 percent of Black students living with both parents (Diamond and Huguley, 2014, p. 754).
- Some 84 percent of US households with school-age children send their children to their assigned traditional public school, and most of the other 16 percent of students enroll in a traditional public school via inter- or intradistrict transfer (Ely and Teske, 2015, p. 179).
- When parents and caregivers consider the selection of a choice school, almost three-fourths investigate a school's academic data, and more than 83 percent of these adults gather information from other parents and caregivers whose children are enrolled in a choice school (Ely and Teske, 2015, p. 180).

[*Authors' Comment:* Parents and caregivers play a critical role in the education of students across the nation and in all types of schools (National Association of School Psychologists, 2014). How schools relay academic proficiency provided by the school is a factor for parents when determining whether a school is "good." If, however, a school or school district obfuscates academic data or camouflages data with catchphrases like "excellent" or "high performing," parents and caregivers can fall prey to fairy tales told when school-marketing overshadows purpose and adequacy.]

The Impact of Standardized Testing

- Policy for academic success promulgated by the State of Florida and based on the results of standardized achievement testing "hopes to have 86 percent of White students at or above grade level in math, but for Black students, the goal is 74 percent" (Worrell, 2014, p. 343).
- Virginia policymakers set passing rates in math and reading that differ from student cohort to student cohort: "'82 percent for Asian students, 68 percent for Whites, 52 percent for Latinos, 45 percent for Blacks and 33 percent for kids with disabilities' (Sanchez, 2012)" (Worrell, 2014, p. 343).

[*Authors' Comment:* Standardized tests dominate depictions of student academic proficiency, and data from these assessments is applied to compare teachers, schools, and school districts. So prevalent is the use of the numbers generated by standardized testing that policymakers and politicians show little concern for the research that demonstrates the abject failure of these assessments to serve any comparative purpose reliably. Statistical hocus pocus performed with results from standardized achievement tests is sleight of hand worthy of Houdini but unworthy of the satisfactory quality that all students deserve from US education.]

Contemporary Purpose and Standardized Testing

- The educationally impotent nature of standardized testing is revealed when assessment results have no impact on deficit thinking of adults. Moreover, these results have a deleterious impact on school improvement and on growth of student learning. The percent of students who earn a passing score from grade level to grade level—as illustrated by standardized testing results from Texas—descends from 86 percent of students passing all tests in third grade to 29 percent of students passing all tests in tenth grade (Garza and Garza, 2010, p. 197).
- Data from 24,867 participants in a secondary school study revealed that "only 14 percent of black 11th graders in this sample reported having taken AP English, compared to 22 percent of whites" (Diamond and Huguley, 2014, p. 754).

[*Authors' Comment:* Not only does US education founder when attempting to evaluate and improve student achievement, but American education often denies the capacity of students of color and students in poverty to engage successfully with challenging academic classes and other opportunities for higher-level learning. Deficit thinking in the form of presumptions about the lack of academic prowess of students of color permeates US schools and society. Deficit-thinking on the part of White school personnel and the failure to valorize the lived experience of students impedes the learning and futures of students already marginalized in US society.]

WHAT DO WE HAVE HERE? IMPLICATIONS FROM THE SELFIE

Implications spring from this data selfie. The first implication is that the historic purpose of public education can no longer suffice if American schools are to deliver "the nation's greatest intentional sustained effort to ensure the promises of American democracy" (Swensson, Ellis, and Shaffer, 2019b).

Pursuit of a primary purpose for US public education is required if adequacy in twenty-first century teaching and learning is to be sufficient to lead-out and engage all students with the cognitive behaviors worthy of their capabilities. Sternberg (2002) calls this *successful intelligence*. "One is successfully intelligent to the extent one effectively adapts to, shapes, and selects environments" (Sternberg, 2002, p. 385).

An additional implication drawn from this selfie is that public education must embrace an amalgam of caring for all students. Family, culture, language, and other elements of the lived experience of students of color and students in poverty too often are marginalized by an overwhelming narrative at school that disdains these assets and the care in a learning community that all students deserve.

Devoid of a primary purpose worthy of the unlimited futures that all US students deserve, the enduring legacy of contemporary education in America is exclusion, the denial of positive liberty (Fraser-Burgess, 2012), and truncated intelligences.

A Picture That Demands at Least a Thousand Words

The implications drawn from the data selfie suggest the question that challenges this search for educational adequacy for the good public school in the twenty-first century: What are the educational factors necessary and sufficient to valorize all students, lead-out all students' capabilities to higher-order cognition, and engage all students with habits of mind that facilitate successful intelligence?

Responding to this challenge is the professional responsibility of all who serve in US public schools. But this responsibility becomes tangled in a contemporary thicket where adequacy of and purpose for public education are lost, abandoned, or denied. Several observations summarize these entanglements and how they affect this search:

- Contemporary teaching and learning in the United States show signs of deterioration fostered by adult-centric advantage. Free market theory is one example of adult-centric advantage and its power to shortchange students, destroy career paths for potential educators, and sustain the nation's devastating legacy of segregation.
- Broken into pieces by publics and perspectives, education in America insufficiently recognizes the value of identity and the unity inherent in valorizing each student's "I identify as . . ." statement. Numerous studies convey the inequitable outcomes and unbalanced expectations delivered to different cohorts of American students (NPR, 2018).
- Fault lines throughout both traditional public education and the free market of schooling seriously undercut educational adequacy.
- Educators in US public schools are in position to make the most of the strengths in lived experience of an impressively diverse student body. The role of relationship-building, care of concern, and social interaction in teaching and learning cannot be overemphasized. The rich resources of each student are located "within multiple cultural contexts simultaneously, at the epicenter of a connected system of circles (e.g., family, school, community) with bidirectional influence (Miranda, 2014)" (Minkos et al., 2017, p. 4).
- The continuous improvement and dynamic instruction established when professional practices are woven within educational function, when social justice is established by valorizing "I identify as . . ." statements, and when traditional public education is defended against ideology are dependent upon educators' pursuing a primary purpose. Without persistent pursuit of a primary purpose, American education spins its wheels while students, communities, and society agonize over a vehicle that's going nowhere.

A FUTURE FOR US PUBLIC EDUCATION

The purpose of contemporary public education and educational adequacy in the United States go hand in hand. As mentioned previously, the perceptions of parents and caregivers often suffice to identify a "good school." Across the nation, however, satisfaction and quality are so incomplete that public education is missing both a primary purpose and a clear sense of adequacy.

Contemporary US public education, as a result, is immobilized. Educational adequacy (defined in terms that create satisfactory quality in all schools for all students) is mired in a contemporary purpose of public schools that ill serves all students and their futures. This state of affairs permits little forward motion for teaching and learning. Adequacy, valorization, and quality contend against adult-centric cross-purposes, perspectives and publics at odds, and misapplication of poorly conceived professional constructs.

Throughout the remainder of this discussion, searching for educational adequacy in the good public school will involve escaping the grip of contemporary purpose. The importance of this effort lies in the understanding that all students who walk into every US classroom are diverse and capable individuals.

This search for the good public school—a comprehensive public education for all students throughout the remainder of the twenty-first century—asks questions and makes assertions that are at odds with firmly held beliefs rooted in the contemporary purpose of public education. These questions and assertions are required because some of these beliefs helped US education become purpose-less and less than adequate in the first place.

BEGINNING TO SEARCH WITH THE END IN MIND

"A good public school prepares students for "the 'unfixed' social world for which young people will be learning" (McWilliam, 2008, p. 264). If this search seeks the nature of educational adequacy and the good public school where all students are prepared for an unfixed world, then this discussion must identify an end in mind, some set of ideas that encompasses educational adequacy and the good public school. To this end, the good public school, the object of this search, is *21CPE* (twenty-first century Comprehensive Public Education).

TWO

True North

The Moral Obligation of Public Education

For a geographer, the term *True North* refers to the northern location of Earth's imaginary axis. Distinct from magnetic north (aka the North Pole), True North cannot be found with the quick spin of a compass needle. Instead, finding True North requires precise calculation, clarity of purpose, adequate skills, engagement of personal characteristics, and agency sufficient to unite and apply these assets.

In everyday conversation, the term *True North* refers to an individual's lifelong journey to find a personal axis represented by fervently sought goals. Scholars recognize True North as a person's life story focused on "a central 'dream' or mission, or an ideal that they want to attain" (Goodson, 2007, p. 132).

Fostered by capabilities, lived experience, race, interests, culture, intelligences, faith, language, gender orientation, needs, family, environments, ethnicity, and aspirations, True North journeys are "provisioned" early and throughout life. Among the supplies for an individual's True North journey are the expectations of the groups, communities, and society of which a person is a part. Often referred to as socialization, learning how to behave to meet expectations of these groups, communities, and society lends meaning throughout each True North journey.

TRUE NORTH AND SOCIALIZATION

US Public education hosts a plethora of communities (e.g., classrooms, individual schools, school organizations/clubs). Socialization is an unavoidable experience within these "complex social settings characterized by social interactions between teachers and students and among students. These interactions serve as socializing agents for children (Tardy, 1985)" (Curby, Rimm-Kaufman, and Abry, 2013, p. 558).

Research confirms the omnipresence of socialization because "students are always learning social, emotional, and ethical 'lessons' from teachers and parents" (Cohen, McCabe, Michelli, and Pickeral, 2009, p. 199). Research also confirms that intellect and academic achievement are fostered during social interaction. This "represents the view that human intelligence has an intrinsically social quality, in that evolution has equipped us with brains that enable us to operate effectively in complex social settings" (Mercer, 2013, p. 148).

Campbell (2008) suggests the impact of this learning when she echoes research findings that "the moral atmosphere that students actually experience in their schools—the manner of their teachers, the integrity of the school codes, the quality of the peer relationships that they form—has more influence on character growth than do academic programs (p. 132)" (p. 609).

The purpose of this chapter is to explore the moral obligation of public education. Because socialization is unavoidable in the communities of public education, this search must attend to integrity and moral atmosphere. True North for US public education cannot be found unless socialization is embraced by responsibility, obligation, and morality.

SOCIALIZATION AND MORAL OBLIGATION IN PUBLIC EDUCATION

Scholars indicate that socialization is one of three interdependent functions of education. These three (socialization, qualification, and subjectification [Biesta, 2009]) represent major outcomes students can expect from educational experiences. How education ensures that students are *qualified* for a productive adulthood, *socialized* to meet the expectations of society, and *subjectified* for new pathways throughout life illustrates overarching effects of what this discussion will refer to as *the original power of education*.

Public education—including, but not limited to, its three interdependent functions—is the responsibility of each of the fifty states. Guided by constitutional provisions for education, each state has control over public education to *lead-out* knowledge and cognitive process where socialization is inevitable. State control of learning and socialization creates a moral obligation.

Moral Obligation: One Point of View

One way to think about the moral obligation of public education emerges in the values it represents, including "overarching principles [that] have been agreed on in our society and within the teaching profession—principles dealing with honesty, fairness, protection of the weak, and respect for all people (Clark, 1990, p. 252)" (Campbell, 2008, p. 602). As these principles illustrate, morality is about interactions that "focus on the effects those actions have upon the welfare of others" (Nucci, 2008, p. 294).

Strike (2008) identifies Occam's Razor, the simplest assumption about this view of moral obligation, when he observes that "education is an initiation into practices and into the communities that sustain them. Initiation into these communities involves learning norms and valuing goods that contribute to the development of a sense of justice" (p. 117).

American public schools, after all, are recognized as "a central institution of democracy—something that sustains democracy but also, in its best forms, is democracy in action" (Stitzlein, 2015, p. 564). Day-to-day fulfillment of a sense of justice during teaching and learning typically occurs in the form of "generalized moral and ethical values relating to how human beings should treat one another (e.g., kindly, fairly, truthfully)" (Campbell, 2008, p. 608).

Moral Obligation: Another Point of View

These principles, however, are not the only point of view about socialization and the moral obligation of US public education. Interpretations engendered by free market schooling assert free market theory, singularity, and what-to-think to fulfill the moral obligation of public education. *Singularity* refers to the moral obligation to pursue the contemporary purpose of education because it fulfills the self-interest of individuals.

The moral obligation of schooling from this point of view is fulfilled through choice education. To ensure that a morality of self-interest proliferates, choice education is construed as mechanisms (e.g., charter schools, vouchers, tax credits). A central part of this belief is that self-interest is fulfilled best when education occurs beyond the stifling overreach of government, in this case represented by traditional public education. The central perception of free market schooling is the view that individual self-interest justifies anything.

THE TROUBLED HISTORY OF MORAL OBLIGATION

Under these conditions, the moral obligation of public education in the United States becomes a creature subject to the vagaries of interpretation within policies and politics aligned with the contemporary purpose of education. A panoply of arbiters (including, but not limited to, legislators, plutocrats, networked ideologues, business leaders, scholars, and educators) echo this purpose and, thus, determine how the moral obligation of US schooling is fulfilled.

Although the moral obligation of public education is a duty to which educators, policymakers, politicians, and citizens are bound by the nature of US democracy and the intentions embedded in universal and free, too often this obligation goes unfulfilled.

The Impact of US History

The history of US education chronicles numerous examples of the abandonment of moral obligation. Aided and abetted throughout America's often nefarious, certainly uneven, approach to the morality inherent in the nation's presumption of justice for all, the realm of US education bears the stain of injustice.

The abandonment of moral obligation, for instance, is nowhere more apparent than when American history and education are under the sway of racism, the moral opposite of "the good." Rector-Aranda (2016) shares a succinct definition of racism as "an uncritical habit of mind (including perceptions, attitudes, assumptions, and beliefs) that justifies inequity and exploitation by accepting the existing order of things as given" (p. 3).

A range of instances of racism litter America's educational history and practice. From resistance to school desegregation to one state's dismantling of its entire public education system in response to *Brown v. Board of Education* (1954), and from segregation academies that ensure all-White student enrollment to school funding mechanisms that create the conditions for state-sponsored segregation (Swensson, Ellis, and Shaffer, 2019b), too many instances demonstrate the ease with which the moral obligation of public education is subverted (Barnum, 2017).

Segregated minority schools suffer the depredations of this moral obligation forsaken: "fewer educational resources such as teacher quality and experience, parent and student resources, stability of enrollment, and advanced instruction" (Orfield and Frankenberg, 2014, p. 719). Marginalizing behaviors such as deficit thinking are chosen by some educators and symbolize the uncritical habits of mind that constitute racism.

Deficit thinking is the baseless assumption that students of color and students in poverty are inherently deficient, unable to perform academically at high levels because of their race, socioeconomic status, culture, ethnicity, language, or other factors (Garza and Garza, 2010). Deficit thinking, research suggests, is far too prevalent. "Public school educators typically operate from a deficit-thinking perspective in regard to children of color" (Garza and Garza, 2010, p. 191). Uncritical habits of mind exemplify the immorality of hate, bigotry, and discrimination. Assuming any student is inferior constitutes an egregious, unacceptable act.

MORAL OBLIGATION AND THE ABSENCE OF CRITICAL HABITS OF MIND

In the absence of critical habits of mind, individual predilections can predominate in classrooms and schools. In the absence of behaviors based on critical habits of mind, natural thinking and meaning-making can exude singularity and self-interest that exclude and marginalize "others." How moral obligation is understood and expressed in schools depends on how critical habits of mind and uncritical habits of mind are woven into teaching and learning.

A failure to recognize, honor, and engage with the intelligences and personal capacities of students of color—depending on the habits of mind "in play" by an educator—represents the damage done by choices that undercut purpose, short-change adequacy, and deny moral obligation. Under these circumstances, students of color pay the heavy price that scholars refer to as *racial opportunity cost* (Chambers, Huggins, Locke, and Fowler, 2014). Racial opportunity cost constitutes the negative effects imposed upon students of color who work to attain academic excellence.

Denial of the capacity and capability of students of color for academic excellence, among the negative assumptions that constitute adults' deficit thinking, reveals the bigotry that fuels this cost. "At issue is not whether a student is actually smart or academically capable, but rather whether their presentation of *smart* and *capable* is judged to be correct" (emphasis original) (Chambers et al., 2014, p. 468).

Costs like these multiply the impacts of *double consciousness* in the lives of students of color. W. E. B. Du Bois identified and decried double consciousness as the ever-present tension of being both Black and an American. This tension—more than a century after Du Bois described it—continues to play a damaging role in contemporary US education because students of color "struggle to express who they are as Black and Latina/o youths while at the same time [they] ascribe to the socially constructed expectations for academic achievement in their schools" (Chambers et al., 2014, p. 467).

Racial opportunity cost is an example of double consciousness in the sense that students of color must pay a price exacted by prejudice and denial. This price entails the denial of academic capability alongside the marginalization of "I identify as . . ." statements. Negative socially constructed expectations fueled by uncritical habits of mind lock students of color in learning environments laden with prejudice where the moral obligation of public education dissolves.

THE CAPACITY FOR MORAL OBLIGATION IN PUBLIC EDUCATION

Scholars recognize a "normative disposition of schools that can either draw out student capacities or constrain them" (Adams et al., 2016, p. 170). The disposition to draw out student capacities to fulfill education's moral obligation lies in the original power of teaching and learning to establish connections "between reasoning and social conventions and moral concepts about fairness and human welfare" (Nucci, 2008, p. 292). These insights foreshadow the necessity of a search for the intersection between *how to think* and the values of moral obligation.

Students enter classrooms ready and able to make connections and choices in relation to moral obligation. On the one hand, students enter all classrooms in possession of a treasure trove of lived experience, natural thinking, and meaning-making. These are foundational capacities to engage in praiseworthy conceptions of "the good." On the other hand, a student's treasure trove of readiness can be directed to accommodate connections among a limited set of ideological frameworks mandated by adult-centric educational choices.

Fulfillment of the moral obligation of public education depends on whether educators (1) *lead-out* student capacities to principled reasoning, and (2) foster *autonomy* and *relatedness*.

Leading-Out Principled Reasoning

Principled reasoning is the amalgam of critical habits of mind that permit any individual to choose to pay the cost of giving up some personal goods to gain the benefit of public goods. Without access to a multitude of habits of mind interplaying with the brain's layers of cognition, however, students are subject to a purpose in public education that entails uncritical habits of mind.

Within the institutional imperative for the moral obligation of public education is the rarely acknowledged necessity that independent thinking is a precursor for emotional intelligence that expresses the values of moral obligation.

Independent thinking is the combination of principled reasoning and positive liberty that facilitates individuals' invocation of the values of moral obligation. Independent thinking is the cognitive agency capable of establishing reciprocity between self-mastery, public liberty, and principled reasoning.

Fostering Autonomy and Relatedness

Adams et al. illustrate that autonomy constitutes a student's belief that she/he "can control their own academic outcomes (Deci and Ryan, 2008)" (Adams et al., 2016, p. 171).

Autonomy embodies independent thinking. Relatedness is a matter of trust in classrooms and schools where "students perceive teachers as sufficiently exhibiting trustworthy behaviors: benevolence, openness, honesty, reliability, and competence (Hoy and Tschannen-Moran, 1999)" (Adams et al., 2016, p. 171). Autonomy and relatedness speak to the need of students to be competent and the value of educators trusting the capability and competence of students.

Autonomy realized and relatedness implemented is a foundation for the cognitive agency of students sufficient to begin to control their academic/cognitive behaviors. Teaching and learning under these circumstances in pursuit of *how to think* invoke the individual freedom of *self-mastery* or *self-regulation*.

Herein lies the power of public education to influence the imperatives of moral obligation: self-mastery or self-regulation. Self-mastery "is the conscious intentional process of gradually taking ownership ('colonizing') of various aspects of the self, including one's emotions, impulses, and dispositions" (Lapsley, 2008, p. 36).

Self-regulation develops in classrooms and schools that support "innate psychological needs—those of autonomy, relatedness, and competence (Ryan and Deci, 2000)" (Adams et al., 2016, p. 170). To engage students in reflection about learning and thinking, *principled reasoning* is the objective of teaching and learning in the intersection of *how to think* and the moral obligation of public education.

It's important to acknowledge that this, or any, discussion about cognitive agency and moral obligation in public education touches on constructs of personality and self. A full explanation of these constructs is beyond the scope of this discussion and is best left to the literature of another discipline (Lapsley, 2008: Nucci, 2008). However, this discussion recognizes the educational applicability of "psychological theories that require conscious, intentional, and volitional self-appropriation and self-mastery" (Lapsley, 2008, p. 47).

This suggests that *leading-out* students' cognitive capacities via principled reasoning to realize cognitive agency invokes aspects of volitional self-appropriation. More simply put, the conjunction of moral obligation and cognitive agency in teaching and learning supports the intentional and conscious "taking over" of ownership of morality by the self—generally thought of as self-mastery (Lapsley, 2008). Self-regulation or self-mastery emerges when students learn to think about their thinking. Self-regulation emerges from "making metacognitive and learning strategies explicit to children and encouraging them to reflect and talk about their learning" (Mercer, 2013, p. 157).

INTERPRETATIONS OF MORAL OBLIGATION

A key is required to unlock the value of collective identity, the freedom in independent thinking, and the capabilities of all students that fulfillment of the moral obligation of public education permits (Ogbu, 2004). This key takes the shape of two imperatives of moral obligation. The value of the key is determined by the capacity of educators to exercise moral obligation through critical habits of mind.

Two Imperatives of the Moral Obligation of Public Education

Fullan (1994) refers to the *institutional imperative* of public schools to fulfill the moral obligation of public education. Four aspects of this imperative are articulated by Goodlad (1990): *facilitating critical enculturation, providing access to knowledge, inquiry, competence, freedom,* and *social justice* (Fullan, 1994, pp. 8–9). These four constitute access to critical habits of mind related to "standards of fairness, the rights of individuals and with regard to accepting and addressing differences among individuals and cultural groups" (Reimers, 2006, p. 280).

The second imperative of the moral obligation of public education is the *moral purpose* of the individual teacher (Fullan, 1994). Moral purpose depends on the habits of mind applied to make choices and decisions in the classroom. "In terms of moral agency and ethical knowledge, what makes teachers' practices morally and ethically meaningful rests on whether core virtues and principles are evidently bound up in their intentions and actions" (Campbell, 2008, p. 606).

The moral obligation of public education in the learning community of each classroom segues with the moral purpose of the teacher (Fullan, 1994). Campbell (2008) indicates that the individual teacher's professionalism cannot be separated from "the teacher's ethical knowledge" (p. 601) and that this ethical knowledge is the synergy between a teacher's morally appropriate conduct and the way the teacher delivers moral education.

Responses to These Imperatives

Responses to these imperatives tend to take one of two paths in contemporary public education. Both paths, ironically, lead to putting students in position "to become good citizens, and if they are to acquire a praiseworthy conception of the good, they must be initiated into communities that function as custodians and transmitters of norms that promote justice and praiseworthy conceptions of the good" (Strike, 2008, p. 121). Defining "the good" becomes central to the moral obligation of US public education.

Both imperatives of moral obligation in public education establish the need for professional practices that engage students with critical habits of mind that facilitate social justice. "Social justice implies that persons have an obligation to be active and productive participants in the life of society and that *society has a duty to enable them to participate in this way*" (emphasis original) (Reisch, 2002, p. 346). The imperatives of moral obligation engage all students with the depth and breadth of principled reasoning necessary and sufficient for *social justice participation that renders the lived experience of every human privileged* (Swensson, Ellis, and Shaffer, 2019b).

STUDENTS AND SELF-MASTERY AND PRINCIPLED REASONING

Public educators who exercise their self-mastery as decisive mechanisms have a profound impact on the moral and cognitive agency of students. Further, teaching that entails self-mastery cannot ignore the societal impediments, racial discrimination, family crises, and other difficulties that forestall learning.

To realize conceptions of the good, the self-regulation of public educators must be the power of moral agency. The importance of this role is captured in comments made by a US senator about public school employees. "We've almost basically asked them to step in where parents, and communities and the social structure of an area hasn't been able to do their job, and do it for them" (Hefling, 2018c).

Students fending for themselves at home, marginalized in society, or assaulted by the consequences of drug addiction, for example, arrive at school in need of care exemplars whose professional practices exemplify moral agency in the form of the educator's self-mastery. "Teachers console children whose parents have died, gone to jail or disappeared as foster care rates increase" (Hefling, 2018c).

In terms of the scourge of drug addiction plaguing communities throughout the United States, public school educators "are on the silent front lines of the epidemic at a time when many already feel overtaxed as a result of budget cuts and chronic shortages of school counselors, psychologists and social workers" (Hefling, 2018c).

Teaching, the mediating influence and professional choices of public educators within educational function, will be referred to in this discussion as *dynamic instruction*. Dynamic instruction entails "the cyclical relation between emotional and instructional supports" (Curby, Rimm-Kaufman, and Abry, 2013, p. 566) that exemplify the professional practices undertaken in the intersection between *how to think* and moral obligation. Studies relevant to dynamic instruction (about which more will be said later) suggest several instructional behaviors that engage students with self-regulation, including cooperative group work, debriefing, self-explanation, and self-assessment (Mercer, 2013).

It's important to the success of this search that the power of self-regulation is understood as a freedom derived from principled reasoning. Educators demonstrate the capacity of public education to fulfill its moral obligation when dynamic instruction *leads-out* principled reasoning, the values of moral obligation, and self-mastery for all students.

CHOICES AND THE FUTURE OF MORAL OBLIGATION

Choices about educational adequacy influence the fulfillment of the moral obligation of public education. Educators must choose whether to *lead-out* the natural thinking of students via engagement with habits of mind. Educators must choose whether to engage students with singularity to fulfill moral obligation in the classroom. The paramount choice for the future of public education is whether this engagement occurs in the intersection of *how to think* and the values of the moral obligation of education.

Choices about crafting this intersection and fulfilling the moral obligation of public education determine whether all students have learning experiences sufficient to attain positive liberty and independent thinking.

Moral Obligation and Choices about Student Capacity

To fulfill the moral obligation of public education, educators must choose to teach with trust in student capacity. Trust in the student's open-ended capacity for meaning-making must imbue choices about instruction with the pursuit of *how to think*. Choosing to pursue the intersection of primary purpose and moral obligation is both trust in and valorization of each student.

Engaging student capabilities with habits of mind *leads-out* meaning-making and individual assets as a foundation for conceptions of the good and respect for others. This is the educators' choice to pursue a primary purpose that yields *principled reasoning*. In this sense, *how to think* engages students with the knowledge and cognitive process necessary for choosing conceptions of the good that are praiseworthy.

Moral Obligation and Choices about Agency in Public Education

Although individual ownership of morality does not lie exclusively within the cognitive domain, moral character grows from alignment between individual assets, the imperatives and values of moral obligation, and traits that include the critical habits of mind pursuant to *how to think* (Lapsley, 2008, p. 36). As this alignment occurs during dynamic instruction, moral agency in US public education is facilitated. Moral agency is expressed in the values of moral obligation chosen via the cognition and behavior (e.g., self-regulation) of educators as "honesty, a sense of fairness, integrity, compassion, patience, respect, impartiality, care, dedication, and other such core virtues" (Campbell, 2008, p. 603).

Moral agency, for the purposes of this discussion, is the interplay between cognition and behavior aligned with the values of the moral obligation of public education necessary for self-mastery during a student's True North journey.

Teachers (who are an example of the individuals in a student's life that studies refer to as *care exemplars* [Lapsley, 2008]) play a critical role in the varied networks that model moral agency for students. Students commit to norms and ideals of morality because the social influence of educators is "a decisive mechanism" (Lapsley, 2008, p. 44).

STANDING IN THE WAY OF MORAL OBLIGATION

When the moral obligation of public education goes unfulfilled, American history records that schools and educators deny the lived experience, competence, and capabilities of students of color and students in poverty. When the moral obligation of public education is forsaken, US schools and educators forsake a professional True North.

The lie of intellectual inferiority linked to race stands as one of the most demeaning, false, and damaging examples of racism to afflict US public education. Extensive literature reveals that "no credible studies have ever suggested that there is an *intelligence gap* (emphasis original), but rather a gap in the ability to demonstrate academic achievement" (Hampton, 2016, p. 440).

The unacceptable, debunked, and racist notion that any racial or ethnic group is academically superior must be countered vigorously with the research that finds no "support for the hypothesized differences in learning styles between African Americans and European Americans (e.g., Boykin, Allen, Hart-Davis, and Senior, 1987)" (Worrell, 2014, p. 335).

Nevertheless, pundits, politicians, policymakers, and scholars are swayed by the unrelieved bigotry of thinking that posits "inequality in the outcomes of schooling is a function of the natural inequality of talent among people (Ornstein, 1977), due to the different mental patterns and thinking processes that are shaped by both genetics and environmental forces" (Eng, 2013, p. 280).

The damage done by unwarranted assumptions of superiority embraced by one community or another lies in what is truly obvious: bias and discrimination in the deliberate erosion of the self-respect of "others" belittles, denigrates, and denies the all-encompassing humanity that is social justice and, thus, disassembles the social contract alongside the demolition of the moral obligation of public education.

The failure to attend to the moral obligation of public education and the failure to attend to *how to think* go hand in hand during the history of American education. Segregation academies established in the aftermath of *Brown v. Board of Education* (1954) and continuing into the twenty-first century, ideological instructional materials used in some choice schools, and active neglect of students in poverty and students of color by traditional public school systems—all are symptoms of imbalance.

Without *how to think* providing the capacity for balance between what's good from the individual's point of view with what's a "public good," people tend to gravitate to what Strike (2008) refers to as "the ethos of the market." The primacy of singularity embedded in this ethos puts the individual in position to calculate only personal "interests (and these may be understood in untutored and unworthy ways) and to see life as a competition for goods, opportunities, and resources. Justice may find it difficult to get a purchase on the soul of such a person" (Strike, 2008, p. 120).

PRECEPTS OF THE MORAL OBLIGATION OF US PUBLIC EDUCATION

The moral obligation of US public education rests within several precepts:

- The moral obligation of public education is to deliver in each school and classroom the elements of teaching and learning necessary and sufficient to equip all US students for a successful journey toward their True North.
- The moral obligation of public education is a necessary consequence of the public's taking responsibility for the education of all children and young people. The fulfillment of moral obligation in the act of educating youth is a non-negotiable in a democracy (Dewey, 1916). The "public" in public education is an expression of diversity that demands teaching and learning without prejudice, discrimination, favoritism, or bigotry.
- The moral obligation of public education is vouchsafed when all students engage with teaching and learning that fosters cognitive behaviors necessary and sufficient to honesty, social justice, public liberty, truth, and the excellence of integrity (Strike, 2008).
- The moral obligation of public educators is to incorporate *ethical/moral purpose* (Fullan, 1994) within all teaching and learning.
- The moral obligation of US public education is to erase historic practices, procedures, and perspectives that prevent equipping all students for ethical travel to their True North. These practices, procedures, and perspectives are barriers that, at the baseline, restrict the freedom that education fosters.

- The moral obligation of public education fosters several research-based outcomes, including that "a highly predictable feature of student achievement is the individual teacher's skill in developing interpersonal relationships with students (Hattie, 2009)" (Mincu, 2015, p. 257).

The denial of competence and capability in educational settings is the denial of social justice because the capacities of human cognition are neither restrained by nor restricted to race, gender, sexual orientation, culture, class, community, socioeconomic status, or any other aspect of lived experience. The harm for students and our society that arises from the loss of True North in public education is the denial of the assets, capabilities, and cognitive strengths of students of color and students in poverty. This loss—in the acts and aura of discrimination found in some schools—sullies US education.

This search for twenty-first century Comprehensive Public Education (*21CPE*) is a hunt for the elements and characteristics of teaching and learning that foster the capabilities all students require to seek their own True North ethically. This search, however, begins encumbered by an anemic purpose for contemporary public education. Stuck in the past, disconnected from the lived experience of too many students, US public education is ineffectual when it comes to understanding and implementing its moral obligation.

A number of barriers stand in the way of fulfilling the moral obligation of public education. These barriers also prevent expression of the original purpose of teaching and learning. The contemporary purpose of public education blocks the construction of an intersection between *how to think* and the fulfillment of moral obligation on behalf of all US students.

Throughout this discussion, the True North journey identified for US public education will follow the path that links *how to think* and moral obligation.

Significant barriers including two perspectives—traditional public education and free market schooling—stand in the way of this search for the good public school. Two publics further obstruct this search for the potential of US education. Dismantling these roadblocks, and several others along the way, is a necessary next step before following the clues that lead to *21CPE*.

THREE
The Eye of the Beholder

An Unavoidable Barrier

The fundamental promises and the potential of US public education go unfulfilled. The promise of universality, where all students are engaged with learning in the intersection between the primary purpose and moral obligation of public education, lies dormant. The promise of freedom is a hit-or-miss proposition because the original power of education is disconnected from too many students. The potential of *how to think* is embargoed by a reactionary purpose. The potential in moral obligation is often forsaken.

US public education is subject to forces and factors that disrupt and deny promises and potential. The mere presence of segregation academies, an archaic purpose, and minimums masquerading as adequacy indicate the extent to which the promises of public education are unfulfilled. The impact of this denial on the lives and futures of all US students puts this search for satisfactory quality, for adequacy, and for the good public school into motion.

THIS SEARCH AND ITS BARRIERS

Barriers must be surmounted before any search begins. This search for the good public school and the educational adequacy at the center of this school is no different. The first of several barriers to be dealt with is *the eye of the beholder*. The goal of this chapter is to explore the two major perspectives and two publics that constitute this imposing obstacle to comprehensive public education.

THE PERSPECTIVES AND PUBLICS OF CONTEMPORARY US PUBLIC EDUCATION

Looking at US public education is like looking through a kaleidoscope: a limited, monocular, viewpoint of confusing collisions in an ever-changing pattern. Views of public education conflict, overlap, separate, dissolve, and swirl. Looking through their own kaleidoscopes at US public education are two major perspectives (traditional public education and free market schools) and two publics (The Public and *the public*). The perspective and public that is chosen determines the viewpoint of the eye of the beholder regarding educational adequacy and the nature of the good public school.

The eye of the beholder views American public education in ways that are blatantly perceiver-centric: allegiances to different methodological prescriptions; regard for personal attributes of individual faculty or school leadership; orthodoxy generated by opposing ideologies and religious persuasions; and/or personal predilections, presumptions, and prejudices.

Partisans of the two perspectives (free market schooling and traditional public education) array their logical, financial, and political weaponry to defeat practices and programs of the "other side." As each kaleidoscope turns, differing educational perceptions ensue, for instance, to declaim either encroaching privatization or the demons of unionization (Reckhow, Grossmann, and Evans, 2015). The distortions endemic to these perspectives multiply when two iterations of the public (The Public and *the public*) create swirling views in their unique kaleidoscopes.

History and the Eye of the Beholder

Anchored originally by clear vocabulary—universal and free—in state constitutions, US public schools are inextricably linked to American history. Segregation, manipulation of funding, disparities between schools, racism, marginalization—all intertwine America's history and its public schools (Goldstein, 2014; US Commission on Civil Rights, 2018).

Language in state constitutions about public education implies a welcome for all students supported by taxpayer funding. But vocabulary is subject to interpretation, legal review, and legislation. Moreover, the eye of the beholder influences the extent of this welcome and public funding for it. "These formalist attributes have been met to varying degrees with a history of funding inequity and practices that discriminate against some populations" (Stitzlein, 2015, p. 566).

Entangled as they are, America's history and education ensure that the eye of the beholder is a limiting influence; schooling, subject to the influence of perspectives and publics via policy and politics, has blinders on. "Unfortunately, politicians, community leaders and other stakeholders are frequently engaged in political battles that give rise to disjointed decisions that do little to eradicate these structural obstacles" (Ikpa, 2016, p. 468).

The eye of the beholder, moreover, is unforgiving of compromise, flexibility, and collaboration. On the one hand, traditional public education is criticized by free market schooling adherents as a bureaucratic monolith endowed with monopoly power (DeAngelis and Erickson, 2018).

Proponents of traditional public education respond with research that indicates that "the reform movement is also determined to underfund and disinvest resources for public schooling so that public education can be completely divorced from any democratic notion of governance, teaching and learning" (Giroux, 2014, p. 351).

From education that intends to serve all US students to public education reserved for selected cohorts of students, and from public schools funded by all citizens to taxpayer funding allocated to religious and private schools, publics and perspectives tend to distort and blur the potential of US public education for all students. The perceptions of those invested in free market schooling or traditional public education and the determinations of The Public or *the public* shape interpretations that handcuff contemporary public education to stasis.

MAJOR PERSPECTIVES ABOUT US PUBLIC EDUCATION

Traditional public education and free market schooling are the two major perspectives about US public education embroiled in a struggle for hegemony. The intensity of this struggle for dominance commits devotees of each perspective to a pursuit of righteousness embedded within their educational prerogatives. The supremacy sought, however, is little more than different versions of tunnel vision. Each eye of the beholder obviates a shared or comprehensive understanding of purpose, educational adequacy, function, and moral obligation in US public education.

Free Market Schooling

Advocates of free market schooling (e.g., choice education, privatization) perceive numerous deficiencies within traditional public education ranging from unaccountable bureaucracies to incompetent leaders and from self-indulgent unions to inept teaching methods. For proponents of a free market perspective, deficiencies throughout traditional public education stand as prime examples of the desperate need for the implementation of choice education (Granger, 2008, p. 217; Reckhow, Grossmann, and Evans, 2015).

In contrast to the perspective of traditional public education, free market schooling is heralded as teaching and learning endowed with "some measure of independence from state and district regulations in exchange for accountability to increase student achievement (Kolderie 1990)" (Stein, 2015, p. 599). Researchers identify this development as part of society's trend toward "the 'privatisation' of much of our social and community life" (Goodson, 2007, p. 136).

This eye of the beholder is focused so intently on singularity for its own sake that choice becomes education and educational adequacy becomes synonymous with choice. Mechanisms, from the perspective of school choice proponents, constitute "the evidence for successful school choice programs" (DeAngelis and Erickson, 2018, p. 249).

Among the mechanisms of choice education, charter schools "are public schools that are allowed to operate with fewer restrictions than typical public schools" (Shaw, 2010, p. 244). Charters are rarely operated by traditional public school districts. Instead, private groups including for-profit corporations or not-for-profit organizations operate most public charter schools (Reckhow, Grossman, and Evans, 2015).

Choosing education in the form of various mechanisms conveys the laserlike priority placed by proponents of free market schooling on reducing government and its cost. School choice is advanced as the remedy for the failures of traditional US public education (Chubb and Moe, 1990; DeAngelis and Erickson, 2018).

Privatization proponents often use a shopping metaphor to illustrate that mechanisms are, unto themselves, education (Stein, 2015). Free market school advocates believe that "more careful shopping by students and parents may be all that is required to spur an educated populace, the public good that is sought through education" (Shaw, 2010, p. 252).

Free market shoppers may avail themselves of additional mechanisms like tax credits and educational savings plans. These allow individuals, corporations, and other entities to make contributions to free market schooling in lieu of taxes that otherwise would support traditional public education. Another popular mechanism offered in the free market of schooling, "vouchers allow children to transfer to private schools, with some public funds being transferred along with the student" (Shaw, 2010, p. 244).

Choice + Mechanisms = Competition in the Free Market

Advocates and shoppers in the free market perceive that privatization/school choice is efficient—lower cost and less government involvement. This allows the free market of schooling to give "families as many choices as possible so that parents could match their children to schools that best fit their needs, whatever those needs may be" (DeAngelis and Erickson, 2018, p. 257).

Choice is offered as an inducement for shoppers and as a feature synonymous with efficiency to demonstrate school quality. From this perspective choice, alone, is the criterion that determines worth or value so that the marketplace of education can "be experienced as a shopping mall where image, packaging, and peer pressure count for more than substance and serious argument" (Strike, 2008, p. 120).

When parents and caregivers choose one school instead of others, another ballyhooed feature of the free market of schooling is facilitated: competition. Choosing one school or abandoning a school in favor of another illustrates how "winning schools" and "losing schools" are identified. Parents/caregivers are encouraged to use standardized test scores as one way to judge which schools should be chosen; competition becomes a feature of the marketplace that also counts for more than primary purpose or moral obligation.

Competition, moreover, is perceived as power from the perspective of free market schooling adherents. Competition is promoted as the power required to raise student achievement when "stronger influxes of demand [occur] through a universal school choice program and price differentiation" (DeAngelis and Erickson, 2018, p. 258). When competition prevails, marketplace adherents see additional benefits in that "students are taught to see themselves as being in competition with others for scarce opportunities and goods" (Strike, 2008, p. 121).

Competition and free market mechanisms, in combination, identify a good school that makes "it less costly for parents to opt out of their residentially assigned public school in order to send their children to the school that better fits their needs" (DeAngelis and Erickson, 2018, p. 248). The promises made about free market schooling—better learning, choice, low cost for private education, competition to weed out "bad" schools— "have enshrined charter schools in positive rhetoric, hailing them as 'laboratories of innovation' (Manna and Ryan, 2011)" (Eastman, 2017, p. 285).

In the Free Market Only the Individual Knows Best

The eye of the beholder in free market schooling perceives singularity as a driving force derived from the belief that "relatively few people are likely to spend time and resources making sure that someone else's education (or health care or justice) is adequate" (Shaw, 2010, p. 242). The marketplace endows only the individual, the shopper, with the capacity to create adequacy. Self-interest, then, is the power that allows mechanisms to define education (Shaw, 2010).

The primacy of self-interest (the singularity couched in the phrase *every man for himself*) means that free market schooling embraces disconnection from the public. Singularity, in this sense, distorts what scholars refer to as "the special human capacity for 'theory of mind' [which] allows us to appreciate that we may have different perspectives and concerns" (Mercer, 2013, p. 163).

Although this theory encapsulates the positive interaction between individual and collective understandings that arise when human beings assess and monitor each other's understanding and common knowledge, singularity and the free market perseverate about the necessity of competition as an antidote for the singularity of others.

Competition and singularity are not necessarily praiseworthy attributes of choice education. Scholars examined the habits of parents/caregivers who searched the characteristics of choice schools online. Even when choice schools make information about student success and achievement available online, "racial composition dominates school choice searches" (Whitehurst, 2017, p. 6). Privatization proponents envision socialization, qualification, and subjectification as educational outcomes resulting from dog-eat-dog competition during which students are divided and the curriculum is differentiated "to meet different individual and group interests and abilities, as other industries have already recognized" (Eng, 2013, p. 282).

The marketplace of schooling operates to disconnect individuals from government overreach manifest as school taxes and compulsory school attendance. From the perspective of free market advocates, individual self-interest is rewarded with a greater good unique to this eye of the beholder: disconnection from the public good (Shaw, 2010).

Government-free education from the perspective of free market schooling delivers accountability because the individual's self-identified, self-justified, and self-evaluated needs are what's best for US society. In this perspective about education, "Accountability is largely an economic concern, where taxpayers seek efficient use of their money and a satisfying rate of return on their investment in children" (Stitzlein, 2015, p. 564).

Moreover, proponents of this perspective indicate that "school choice programs diminish monopoly power held by traditional public school leaders and, therefore, lead to increased overall quality levels and lower costs (Chubb and Moe, 1990, Friedman and Friedman, 1990)" (DeAngelis and Erickson, 2018, p. 250).

Privatization proponents see no value in the public good symbolized by traditional public education because "no one has a strong incentive to make sure that the public good is well provided" (Shaw, 2010, p. 242). In free market terms, privatization/choice education offers the incentive that matters: "Maximum output and efficiency by an organization can best be accomplished if there is an opportunity to make a profit; and we should encourage private vendors to enter public education with the profit motive in mind to increase productivity" (Brown, 2002, p. 105).

To Create the Marketplace Only the Self-Anointed Know Best

The free market perspective is supported by a host of networked organizations, foundations, and plutocrats whose elaborate funding efforts support the eye of the beholder dedicated to implementing self-serving, self-aggrandizing principles of free market theory.

Entities including the Cato Institute, the American Legislative Exchange Council (ALEC), the John William Pope Center for Higher Education Policy, the Mercer Foundation, the Heritage Foundation, the Fordham Foundation, the Foundation for Economic Education, the Walmart Foundation, and the Manhattan Institute for Public Policy Research, among others, bankroll policy and legislative initiatives that establish mechanisms of choice education (Granger, 2008; Shaw, 2010; Swensson, Ellis, and Shaffer, 2019a).

These entities promote "privatization of public elementary and secondary education [which] is designed to satisfy political motives and also improve education by injecting market incentives into the system" (Brown, 2002, p. 100). Free market schooling proponents deploy choice and competition as rhetorical battering rams against "public K–12 education [which] is a one-size-fits-all system that is unable to serve students' varied needs" (DeAngelis and Erickson, 2018, p. 250).

A "one for all" approach to US education, aided and abetted by ALEC (American Legislative Exchange Council) in the form of "model bills," is the objective of the networks and foundations that allege a one-size-fits-all impact of traditional public education. ALEC and the other entities proclaiming the superior value of privatization invoke the discredited and unconstitutional approach of "separate but equal" in education without bothering with "equal."

Creating a "one for all" approach by writing educational legislation templates into which legislators need only insert the name of their state, ALEC shares examples of legislation that give privatization proponents "cover" to provide what appears to be a free, universal, and appropriate education.

However, as DuFour and Marzano (2011) illustrate, the myopia of separate pools ideological options instead of "providing people with access to the resources that enable them to make informed decisions" (p. 204). Templates and fill-in-the-blank legislation ensure that both The Public and members of *the public* are entangled in minimums. Moreover, the importance of using evidence about high-quality teaching and learning "to inform and improve rather than demean and punish" (DuFour and Marzano, 2011, p. 205) is ignored when legislation that imposes choice education is the equivalent of microwaveable sausage.

During the early years of choice education in the United States, relatively few privatized schools operated on a for-profit basis. Currently, the funding follies of free market schooling fixate on the money to be made even when choice schools operate on a not-for-profit basis. "Venture capital firms and hedge fund managers began to view nonprofit charter schools as a 'largely untapped and potentially lucrative market'" (Eastman, 2017, p. 286).

Often grouped as networks, for-profit choice schools (including virtual schools) are eligible for tax dollars on a per-pupil basis. In some cases where states imposed limitations—charter schools in several states are prohibited from operating as for-profit enterprises (Eastman, 2017)—entrepreneurs adopted what amounts to an indirect profit pathway. "The private sector started funding for-profit EMO's [education management organizations] to contract with and operate nonprofit charter schools" (Eastman, 2017, p. 287).

Additional profit is available to EMOs. Often, EMOs charge rent for the facility in which the otherwise not-for-profit choice school operates. State funding ends up, once again, in the pockets of for-profit businesses that, in some cases, are "redirecting funds allocated to teacher salaries and resource development to charge charter schools inflated rent for their facilities" (Eastman, 2017, p. 288).

Traditional Public Schools

Nearly 90 percent of students in the United States attend traditional public schools. State constitutions imply that traditional public or common schools serve as a place "where individuals pursue their own liberties while simultaneously upholding those of others" (Stitzlein, 2015, p. 567). Reflecting a theoretical balance summoned by the standards and time-honored vocabulary of US democracy (universal and free), traditional public education is endowed with the potential to serve equitably as both a source and an iteration of the public good.

The public good envisioned by this eye of the beholder is the imperative of democracy to express and expand a balance between equality of opportunity for all and individual freedoms. This imperative facilitates what several researchers reference as "democratic equality—in membership—[which] was essential to prevent the emergence of partial societies within the state that would undermine the common good" (Reimers, 2006, p. 283).

In accordance with the content of state constitutions, traditional public schools welcome all students and strive to meet the multiple needs of all who enroll. Traditional public schools are expected to "be all things to all people by virtue of their open and equitable employment and enrollment guidelines" (Stitzlein, 2015, p. 565).

A wide range of colleagues in traditional public education—for example, social workers, guidance counselors, special education professionals, home-school advisors, occupational and physical therapists, English-language-learning teachers, speech pathologists—augment teachers, paraprofessionals, and school leaders in response to the wide range of these expectations and to the needs of all students.

This perspective, however, delivers a hit-or-miss implementation of its intents and constitutional underpinnings. History is replete with the failures of traditional public education to serve all children. These failures range from cheating on standardized testing to mismanagement of public funds, and from deficit thinking to dismal instruction. Traditional public education is a perspective subject to the negative effects of kaleidoscopic vision.

TWO PUBLICS IN US PUBLIC EDUCATION

Two publics also play starring roles in US education. The first of these will be referred to in this discussion as The Public (always capitalized). The second of these will be referred to in this discussion as *the public* (always italicized).

The Public

The Public represents entities endowed with the constitutional and/or legislative authority for public education. State legislatures, state agencies, the US Congress, and other authorities are The Public. The Public, in theory, has the responsibility for building "an inclusive egalitarian political society comprised of individuals who are constructed as rights-bearing citizens" (Knight Abowitz, 2011, p. 471).

In practice, authorities that comprise The Public are heavily involved in policies, procedures, and practices at the heart of American public education. The Public exercises "symbolic power through the derivation of constitutional principles used to make school governance decisions. These principles are based on values of individual liberty, equality of opportunity, and participatory governance" (Knight Abowitz, 2011, p. 467).

And *the public*

By contrast, the second of the publics referred to throughout this book as *the public* evinces "more organic and episodic eruptions of public will and social movement that form in response to shared problems or problematic situations" (Knight Abowitz, 2011, p. 468).

The public comes on stage when educational issues prompt dialogue about, or attempts to solve, issues and problematic situations in public education. Constituted as previously affiliated groups or among otherwise spontaneously assembled individuals or groups, *the public* weighs in about issues at individual schools and about problems in education nationwide. *The public* usually has no predetermined or precluded membership unless, for example, consideration is given to the fact that most participants in a band boosters organization are parents/caregivers of students in the band.

The interests and concerns of *the public* about public education garner attention and analysis. For example, parents and caregivers of all races, ethnicities, and socioeconomic status reveal in surveys "that the academic quality of schools is at the top of their list of important characteristics (e.g., Armor and Peiser, 1998; Kleitz et al., 2000; Schneider and Buckley, 2002; Smrekar, 2009; Stein et al., 2011)" (Stein, 2015, p. 602).

The Public and *the public* converge in local governance of public education. Voting for a board of education places *the public* in position to exercise democratic authority over The Public. Beyond local governance, *the public* elects state legislators and in so doing presumably can bring The Public to attend to a perspective valued by the electorate. When The Public is not local, however, the influence of *the public* on education fades.

BARRIERS ARISE WHERE NONE SHOULD EXIST

The two major perspectives and the publics wrangle over public education. Student-centric purpose, clarity about educational adequacy, and fulfillment of moral obligation are among the significant matters in dispute. Agreements among and between perspectives and publics about these points of view come and go. The eye of the beholder facilitates the construction of several sturdy walls, barriers daunting for their capacity to isolate, obstruct, and divide:

- *Competition*—Competition siphons funding away from traditional public education. Hidden behind competition is not only denial of enrollment for any reason but also inadequate instruction, measurement, and purpose (Brown, 2002; DeAngelis and Erickson, 2018).
- *Self-perpetuation*—Survival of the fittest and this-is-the-way-we've-always-done-things express how perspectives and publics ensconce self-perpetuation of ideology and institutions as the baseline for public education. Self-perpetuation ensures that conventional wisdom, inadequacy, and stasis abound in US education.
- *Exacerbation*—The Public exacerbates—via policy, funding, and legislation—the internecine warfare between perspectives. The Public further exacerbates the scope and damage done by this warfare when it responds to influence generated by the organizational field instead of engaging with the influence of *the public*.
- *Denial*—The Public, pundits, and plutocrats often deny the value of pedagogy. Denial of the capacities of students of color and students in poverty justifies denial of the value of dynamic instruction to construct the intersection of *how to think* and the moral obligation of

public education for all students. Denial of the original power of education justifies the erroneous assertion that mechanisms are education.

With so many walls between and among perspectives and publics, little continuity and even less adequacy develops within contemporary public education. With little held in common, two perspectives and two publics fail to perceive a primary purpose for US public education. The nature of the good public school and how this appellation might be determined for the twenty-first century is blocked when perspectives and publics obstruct educational adequacy sufficient and necessary for a student-centric purpose in US education.

Why Do These Barriers Endure?

Rarely do common points of view about American education arise among and between perspectives and publics. Scholars observe that "the absence of a science of positive school attributes has limited the design and selection of improvement tools to tired external controls and interventions that do little to build capacity (Darling-Hammond, 2005; Hargreaves, 2011)" (Adams et al., 2016, p. 170).

In large measure, rancorous and retrograde-dependent determinations divide perspectives and publics. Counterproductive perceptions craft policy, ideological purity, funding, and/or political leverage into the barriers that prevent the introspection and investigation required to identify the good public school.

Several questions must be asked if the barriers envisioned by the eye of the beholder are to be removed:

- *Can US public education jettison its jobs-placement purpose?* Ensuring educational adequacy necessary and sufficient to answer to this question begins with accounting for the damage done to students by achievement-lite learning and indifference to moral obligation embedded in the contemporary purpose of US education. This purpose is the cement that binds numerous walls constructed at the behest of the eye of the beholder.
- *Can the charade of providing education via mechanisms end?* The various dysfunctional effects of mechanisms include (1) limiting or excluding student enrollment (e.g., segregation academies continue to exist as the third decade of the twenty-first century begins); (2) dissolving representative democracy for school governance; and (3) purporting that efficiency is tantamount to education. Public education that serves all students in common is a forgotten vision.
- *Can publics* (The Public and *the public*) *and perspectives* (free market schooling and traditional public education) *own up to their responsibility for public education that establishes adequacy beyond minimums?*

Barriers to satisfactory quality exist when the horizon envisioned in the eye of the beholder is only inches away.
- *Is it possible to engage with a primary purpose for teaching and learning and understand that divergent expectations and wayward goals intertwined with the conflicting interests and demands of both publics and both perspectives will continue?* The capabilities engendered via public education pursuing *how to think* (including the cognitive behaviors necessary and sufficient to choose to pay the price of relinquishing some individual predilections in favor of the public good) can sustain the interplay, critique, and diversity of democracy.

TAKING THIS SEARCH BEYOND THE EYE OF THE BEHOLDER

Students marginalized by society pay debilitating costs when subjected to purpose and educational adequacy dependent upon the eye of the beholder. Learners perceived as prefabricated cogs for a needy jobs-placement engine, or subjected to mechanisms masquerading as education, or marginalized by the assumption that minimums establish adequacy become educated in name only.

When this search is taken beyond the eye of the beholder, it is not possible to ignore the fact that perspectives and publics will be involved forever with US public education. For the purposes of this search, then, looking beyond the eye of the beholder requires recognizing that it's neither desirable nor possible to exclude publics and perspectives from the future of US public education.

Eliminating the mountainous barriers established when the eye of the beholder sees only contemporary iterations of educational adequacy, however, is essential if perspectives and publics are to perceive the worth of comprehensive public education. To accomplish this goal, it is necessary to change the lens that limits contemporary US education to a focus on the singularity of individual advantage and preparation for employment realities that no longer exist.

Because publics and perspectives always will play a role in US public education, this search moves forward to locate common ground for public education. For such a promising development to occur, three additional barriers must be dealt with. These three barriers—the tyranny of either/or, conventional wisdom, and measurement—cannot remain in place if this search for the good public school is to succeed.

FOUR

A Barrier Within

The Tyranny of Either/Or

Delineated in the constitutions of all fifty states, the concept of free public education available universally is a noble, novel, American invention. As portrayed in Indiana's constitution, for example, it is the state legislature's duty to "provide, by law, for a general and uniform system of Common Schools, wherein tuition shall be without charge, and equally open to all" (Indiana Constitution, 1851, Article 8). Guaranteed to all in relatively simple language, US public education springs from clear expectations: universal and free.

Thus enshrined, these simple standards fall prey to what this discussion refers to as the *tyranny of either/or* (TEO). Granger (2008) illustrates the depth and breadth of this tyranny metaphorically: "Either/or language and logic both allow for and encourage something like the simple thumbs-up/thumbs-down crowd response of Roman gladiator matches" (p. 211).

Perspectives and publics stake their separate claims throughout public education and revel in the forced choice imposed through TEO. As contemporary views and values in US public education reveal, adequacy and purpose are confined to understandings and practices devoted to "either" or to "or."

THE SYNERGY OF STRUGGLE

The ease with which proponents of the separate perspectives, and representatives within the divided publics, extol and protect their "either" and disdain "or" demonstrates how the tyranny of either/or is propped up by the *synergy of struggle* (Granger, 2008).

The synergy of struggle permits adherents of one perspective or the other to relish the experience of "emotional depth as well as the intellectual satisfaction that springs from the transformation of uncertainty, ambivalence, and complexity into an understandable phenomenon (Edelman, 1988, p. 40)" (Granger, 2008, p. 212). Creating self-serving mantras like these engages proponents of each perspective with an idiographic satisfaction that broaches no critique while it self-justifies. Satisfaction is guaranteed, doubt is assuaged, and uncertainty is reduced.

Critics of traditional public education, for example, find solace in condemning teacher unions and top-heavy school bureaucracies (Chubb and Moe, 1990; Shaw, 2010). Traditional education proponents rail against mandates for America's schools, including "expanding audit culture" and "'quality indicators [that] consist of self-evident truths'" (Granger, 2008, p. 215).

As adults find satisfaction in each thumbs-up for their preferred perspective and justification in each thumbs-down for the notions of the "other" perspective, students receive nothing more than a thumbs-down because the synergy of struggle substantiates a focus on "vulnerabilities, problems, and needs rather than resilience, strengths, and assets (e.g., Kaufman et al., 2007; Novins et al., 2004; Smith et al., 2000)" (McMahon, Baete Kenyon, and Carter, 2013, p. 694).

Under the influence of TEO, and within the infatuations nurtured by the synergy of struggle, the complexities of public education are reduced to proscriptions. This ensures that connection and balance throughout US education are rare. Worse, this state of affairs ensures that conflict is inevitable over the command of educational funding, policy, and power that implement the "correct" and understandable perspective. Tyranny and the synergy of struggle are additional walls throughout US public education that obstruct agreement about a primary purpose (Reckhow, Grossmann, and Evans, 2015).

Characteristics of the Tyranny of Either/Or

Advocates of both traditional public education and free market schooling deploy the characteristics of TEO in the battle for supremacy in American education. The characteristics of TEO are reactionary in the sense that they reinforce practices and perceptions that sustain a future riveted to the limitations of one perspective or another for US public education. These characteristics—*adult-centric advantage, ideology is destiny, reform is ideology,* and *education is singularity*—detain America's public education in a sturdy defense of "either" to ensure the demise of "or."

Adult-Centric Advantage

Adult-centric advantage is decision making, policy, and/or behavior that prioritizes advantages for adults in US public education. Establishing adult advantage within public education is neither simple, nor, on the face of it, justifiable.

Adult-centric advantage seeks efficiency, choice, competition, less government, and less cost. The tyranny of either/or superimposes adult-centric advantage as "either" on public schooling. The result is that the "either" of this advantage rules out any "or," including valorizing students or with engaging all students with higher order achievement. A preoccupation with adult-centric advantage mesmerizes those who seek it and puts those who understand its limitations in the role of "or."

The practical effect of an adult-centric focus is often the marginalization of the lived experience of students in poverty and students of color. For instance, the adult-centric advantage of privilege is a self-satisfaction that prevents valorization of student capacities.

When this condition prevails, adult-centric advantage too readily turns away from virtues of lived experience, including (here confirmed in research focused on American Indian [AI] youth) that "the strengths of AI youth, personal attributes, positive/supportive relationships, and AI culture were found to be significant mechanisms of strength and resilience (Filbert and Flynn, 2010; Montgomery et al., 2000; Stiffman et al., 2007)" (McMahon, Baete Kenyon, and Carter, 2013, p. 264).

Profit, also, is an adult-centric advantage. Companies, politicians, and entrepreneurs, among others, reduce education to understandable cures and gimmicks that earn the satisfying return of profit. Profit, however, has little to do with satisfactory quality in teaching and learning. It does offer, of course, innumerable temptations to make the major perspectives about American public education understandable from a corporate point of view.

Ideology Is Destiny

Ideology is destiny is the contemporary assumption that one professional ideology or the other is the destiny of teaching and learning. Seeking destiny in this way frequently involves "'political competition between two competing advocacy networks and coalitions that want to expand or constrain school choice'" (Reckhow, Grossmann, and Evans, 2015, p. 208). Destiny lies in the ascendency of one educational ideology over the other.

The metaphor of professional wrestling conveys the good-guy or bad-guy dichotomy that anchors ideology to destiny (Granger, 2008). Moreover, investment in this manifestation of TEO anchors public education to an ideology of its own: being a proponent of a perspective means being "right" (aka, the good guy) in opposition to "wrong" (aka, the bad guy) and without regard to what might be held in common between the two on behalf of students. Ideology is exclusionary to the point that destiny is realized only through competition and defeat of the "bad guy."

In the long run, ideology is destiny suggests the validity of the observation that "too much of what passes for change in education is nothing more than moving things around in the hope that things will get better for children" (Brown, 2002, p. 105).

Reform Is Ideology

Perhaps the most prominent element of TEO in play throughout the realm of public education is the invocation of *reform is ideology*. Claiming the mantle of reform stipulates that US public education requires reforming. In addition, assuming that reform is required indicts the "or," the bad guy, as unworthy or harmful. Reform becomes ideology when it becomes what's required to "right" a "wrong." Reform as ideology is the ultimate good guy.

Identifying this good guy, however, is facile. What comprises reform, whether reform is about students and whether reform is a good guy depends on the restrictions inherent in the either/or of ideology. Dependence on this dichotomy sharpens the eye of the beholder. The synergy of struggle nurtures perceptions that a good guy, when all is said and done, seeks change because it thwarts the ideations of "or," an ideological bad guy.

Reform becomes an ideology unto itself. Standards or practices that conform to this ideology earn an automatic "thumbs up" from true believers. Ideological purity justifies adult-centric advantage. Efficiency, competition, and choice, as a result, earn a "thumbs up" as iterations of reform even when they deliver marginalization, profit, and segregation (Swensson, Ellis, and Shaffer, 2019a).

Education Is Singularity

As things stand in contemporary US public education, either public education answers to the singularity of individual good or to the public good. The individual good is appended to education via TEO in the conviction that "if the definition of quality is unique to each individual, we could say that the school selection itself—the student-school match—is the definition of quality" (DeAngelis and Erickson, 2018, p. 251). This circular ethos is the affirmation of an ideology that evokes the necessity of reform in public education dedicated to self-interest.

Public education is singularity when expressed as an "either" that benefits only individuals able to afford it (through government support or through personal wealth) and those individuals lucky enough to live near an adequately funded school. Singularity is manifest when schools and school districts are subject to funding that is an either/or commodity. The "or" standing outside of this market and opposite singularity is the public good.

Ominously, when education is singularity, racism and discrimination hold forth. The past and present of US public education are replete with examples where more funding, better teachers, and higher-level classes advantage schools where most students are White. The "or" in this example of education is the neglected schools that serve students of color and students in poverty (Buszin, 2012–2013). Singularity is intentional exclusion and marginalization in US education.

THE TEO BARRIER: SCHOOL ATTACHED OR SCHOOL DETACHED

The barrier that TEO presents to this search for educational adequacy is daunting because practices in schools and classrooms can reflect either/or assumptions about student capabilities. These TEO-affiliated assumptions about students will be referred to in this discussion as either *school attached* or *school detached*.

School attached is the assumption that a student has the capacities required to engage in and be successful at learning. *School detached* is the assumption that a student does not have the capacities required to engage in learning.

These assumptions are devoid of research, data, or the original power of education. Instead, these assumptions are nothing more than adult discrimination against a student's race, gender identity, religion, language, culture, and/or other aspects of any "I identify as . . ." statement. The viability of a student's power of meaning-making, capabilities enriched by lived experience, capacities for *how to think*, and multiple iterations of intelligence are held hostage when these adult assumptions enforce the tyranny of either/or. The assumption of school detached is an example of *deficit thinking*.

Assuming any student is school attached or school detached has the effect of students being dealt with as if they are either of-community or not-of-community when instruction occurs. Students trapped in these prejudice-originated categories experience teaching and learning walled off by TEO into higher-order cognition or lower-order cognition sectors.

Under these circumstances, education becomes an exclusionary experience where significant cohorts of students are perceived to be beyond or outside the community (Felton, 2018a). Students excluded in this way are marginalized by uncritical habits of mind that perceive "others" as less, unworthy, and deniable. When school-detached educational practices arise, morality disappears and the paradox evolves where the primacy of self-interest is perceived as freedom for the school-attached individual.

The Bricks in This Barrier

The bricks that comprise this barrier not only deter this search for educational adequacy but also reveal the flaws of the contemporary purpose of public education. Understanding this barrier is a key to disengaging US public education from TEO:

- The contemporary purpose of public education is an "either" that permits no "or." Positing students as cogs being prepared for placement in an employment machine, public education falls prey to both market failure and employer bias. Market failure, in this case, is the inability of both educators and the employment market to foresee the future. This failure and employer bias illustrate the tendency of business and industry to blame public education for an alleged dearth of qualified employees when employers are responsible for inadequate pay, benefits, and other job-related inducements. The contemporary purpose of public education fosters preparation for an inchoate job's future.
- The elements of TEO are a Sargasso Sea in which US public education is trapped with no hope of sailing out. Adult-centric and welded to singularity, the tyranny of either/or prevents public schooling that is comprehensive and student-centric. Moreover, the dead end established by the assumption of "right" and nurtured by the synergy of struggle prohibits improvement and a purpose that engages students with whatever their futures may bring.
- The "good guy" or "bad guy" cartoon that plays out between and among perspectives and publics renders maximums for educational adequacy and the moral obligation of public education moot. The internecine warfare that typifies interactions about US public education distracts all perspectives and publics from determining what ought to be held in common to ensure educational adequacy for all US students.
- The barrier created by TEO fosters an all-or-nothing ethos where defending "either" and attacking "or" encourages singularity, self-interest, and disconnection at the expense of educational adequacy, moral obligation, and educational function.

DISMANTLING THE TYRANNY OF EITHER/OR

Considered together, the elements of TEO comprise the barrier known as *ROI* (Return on Investment). ROI embodies the premise that efficiency, profit, and low-cost government are the fiduciary, adult-centric returns expected when society invests in adult-centric advantages to establish public education. ROI reflects the shallow purpose of contemporary public education (Swensson, Ellis, and Shaffer, 2019a).

ROI delivers the expectations of its proponents when choice, mechanisms, and the primacy of singularity are the minimums that suffice for educational adequacy. Once these characteristics are labeled as efficiency, an ideological "either" is created. At the bottom line, when ROI is sought from public education, the beneficiaries are exclusively those who invest in adult-centric advantage.

The apparent invincibility of ROI—policy, funding, and legislation add to this impression—makes TEO a significant barrier to the future of US public education. There is, however, another way to perceive a "return" from public education: Return to Students (RTS). Return to Students invests in the intersection of *how to think* and moral obligation on behalf of all US students as the baseline for the future of teaching and learning in public education (Swensson, Ellis, and Shaffer, 2019a).

The worth of RTS is found in the expression of intelligences shared in the independent thinking evinced when students engage in learning experiences crafted in this intersection. Independent thinking demolishes the barriers of TEO and the synergy of struggle. This expression of intelligences engages students with the capacity "to convert conflicts that are threatening to dissolve the basis for political association into conflicts in which the legitimacy of the other's position is acknowledged" (Knight Abowitz, 2011, p. 477).

RTS orients US public education away from disconnections endemic to singularity and provides public education with a focus on universality of benefit to all students. RTS means that adequacy begins with the freedom that develops from "a more direct focus on improving thinking-skill performance" (Beyer, 2008a, p. 196). Breaking down the barrier created by the tyranny of either/or means embracing a primary purpose for public education that grows the cognitive behaviors of all who enter public school classrooms.

FIVE
Confronting the Barrier of Conventional Wisdom

Conventional wisdom about contemporary US public education is like a tweet. Conventional wisdom shares complex concepts about public education with the same glib certainty and with the same dubious accuracy of any tweet about an issue of substance. From purpose to measurement, from teaching to learning, conventional wisdom suppresses satisfactory quality in contemporary public education with misinformation, misdirection, and manufactured simplicity. The difficult task of overcoming conventional wisdom is suggested by the enduring presence of "learning style" in the popular and pedagogical lexicon despite any research to verify this concept as a viable educational premise (Brown, Roediger, and McDaniel, 2014).

Further evidence of the failure of educators, policymakers, politicians, pundits, and citizens to succeed in overcoming this misconception lies in the fact that no research supports the bigotry of "the hypothesized differences in learning styles between African Americans and European Americans (e.g., Boykin, Allen, Hart-Davis, and Senior, 1987)" (Worrell, 2014, p. 335).

Conventional wisdom is a disservice to satisfactory quality in teaching and learning across the nation. The intent of this chapter is to confront the tweetlike vacuity and damaging impact of conventional wisdom.

THE AUTHORITY OF CONVENTIONAL WISDOM

Conventional wisdom does not derive its authority in American education from any statute or constitutional verbiage. Instead, conventional wisdom is the power of collective agreement about assumptions and "taken for granted" generalizations.

Human beings generate the authority of conventional wisdom because we tend to respond to, think like, and act in accordance with the social influence of friends, family, associated groups, and networks (Hart, 1991). Conventional wisdom develops in this crucible where presumptions, myths, and unverified general knowledge fire the imagination and an allegiance to conventional wisdom offered through social influence.

The negative impact of conventional wisdom is often a devastating marginalization multiplier in the lives of US students. School detached is an example of conventional wisdom that devastates students of color and students in poverty with the assumption that these learners are incapable of academic competence and school success. In response to this baseless conventional wisdom, students of color (given that they realize they have been categorized in this way) detach themselves from school environments and/or adults who make this assumption (Garza and Garza, 2010; Hampton, 2016).

Decisions, practices, and processes tied to conventional wisdom also have the power to deny. Deficit thinking—a baseline of hate—about students of color and students in poverty illuminates the harm created when conventional wisdom is steeped in fear, bigotry, and discrimination arising from racist assertions facilitated via TEO.

THE BALEFUL STATE OF EDUCATIONAL ADEQUACY

When it comes to US public education, *adequate* is a term that ought to connote the satisfactory quality at the foundation of a good public school. Parents and caregivers expect that public education is adequate, at least. But contemporary conventional wisdom about educational adequacy—generated by social networks and within the judicial system—threatens students with enervating, lackluster, purposeless teaching and learning. Satisfactory quality for all students is hard to find because present-day wisdom about educational adequacy is inadequate.

Educational Adequacy as a Social Construction

Conventional wisdom about educational adequacy emerges from what amounts to a construction process. Social influence builds a tautology: *my friend/family member says that's a good school; so, it is a good school* (Ely and Teske, 2015). These social networks are highly influential and unite educational adequacy with conventional wisdom.

Studies capture this convergence where, for instance, "social constructions of 'good' schools for high-status families and the process by which these rankings are perpetuated through class- and race-defined social networks (Brantlinger et al., 1996; Holme, 2002; Johnson and Shapiro, 2003)" (Roda and Wells, 2013, pp. 282–83).

Educational Adequacy as Minimum Quality

Social influence establishes a common eye-of-the-beholder view of educational adequacy. Adequacy from this point of view is subject to misperception, ideological righteousness, and/or myopia. But this blurry vision of an adequate public education is 20/20 eyesight compared with legal views of educational adequacy.

The legal system's vision is rooted in the unenumerated status of education in the US Constitution. This status ensures that provisions for public education are a feature of the constitutions in all fifty states. Further, the US Supreme Court, in *San Antonio Independent School District v. Rodriguez* (1973), declared "that education is not a fundamental right under the U.S. Constitution" (Umpstead, 2007, p. 285). This means that legal challenges to the adequacy of teaching and learning in US public schools are heard in state courts.

A Challenge to Educational Adequacy? See You in Court!

Legal challenges to educational adequacy call for judicial determinations about deficiencies in education and/or disparities between learners. To reach a determination about any of these challenges, courts take into account one of three types of provisions for public education in a state's constitution: establishment provisions, quality provisions, or high duty provisions (Buszin, 2012–2013; Umpstead, 2007, p. 289).

Establishment provisions (in seventeen state constitutions) do not detail the intended quality of education but only that the legislature must create and sustain a free public school system (Buszin, 2012–2013). *Quality provisions* (in eighteen state constitutions) "require the legislature to create a system of public education that is 'thorough,' 'efficient,' or 'thorough and efficient'" (Buszin, 2012–2013, p. 1622). Fourteen constitutions provide that the legislature has a *high duty for education*, which means education is a priority that comes before all other legislative duties (Buszin, 2012–2013).

Judicial consideration of these provisions intersects with three benchmarks—funding, goals, and/or accountability for outcomes (Umpstead, 2007). Provisions and benchmarks provide the courts with the legal wherewithal to gauge the effect of alleged deficiencies and disparities on the adequacy of education provided in a public school system.

Deficiencies and Disparities

Court challenges to educational adequacy are brought to expose deficiencies such as "insufficient numbers of trained teachers, large class size and high student-teacher ratios, shortages of school staff, inadequate educational supplies, scarce equipment, limited course offerings, [and] inadequate curricula or teaching of basic subjects" (Umpstead, 2007, pp. 293–94).

Disparities between student cohorts include, but are not limited to, achievement gaps between racial, socioeconomic, and first-language student cohorts; gaps imposed by racial, SES, and ethnic inequalities in society; funding gaps between wealthy and poor school districts; and gaps between the expectations (for academic proficiency, behavior, language, dress) held by school districts, individual schools, and teachers for various cohorts of students (Garcia and Weiss, 2015).

Data from the school district being challenged and national research findings can play an evidentiary role in court proceedings. For example, if accountability for outcomes is at issue, national research findings reveal that "the academic performance of an average black or Hispanic student [on standardized tests] is equivalent to the performance of an average white student in the lowest quartile of white achievement" (Buszin, 2012–2013, p. 1627).

Research has the potential to augment a challenge to adequacy in a specific school district. For instance, national data demonstrates that across the United States, "poor, minority students generally are taught by the least qualified teachers and are put in classes that teach the least challenging curriculum" (Buszin, 2012–2013, p. 1613). Studies also indicate that teachers hold lower academic expectations for students of color and that "teachers tend to provide less classroom support to minority students than to white students" (Buszin, 2012–2013, p. 1628).

HOW EDUCATIONAL ADEQUACY BECOMES CONVENTIONAL WISDOM

A casual glance at court challenges to educational adequacy could tempt an observer to believe that challenges to satisfactory quality in public education are substantively addressed by state courts. Studies reveal that these venues frequently demonstrate "a willingness to find a state constitutional guarantee to an equal or minimally adequate education" (Buszin, 2012–2013, p. 1631).

A closer look, however, reveals a profound dilemma: educational adequacy is determined using a counterintuitive legal definition. Varied legal considerations and foundational elements—constitutional provisions, consideration of benchmarks, substantive and relevant data—amount to nothing when a desperately fragile definition of educational adequacy handcuffs adjudication of challenges to satisfactory quality.

The Paradox of Educational Adequacy

Fragility and paradox suffuse the contemporary definition of educational adequacy. Fragility, first, is embedded in educational adequacy because state constitutions give authority for public education to state legislatures. As a result, state courts often determine that they have no business adjudicating provisions and/or benchmarks relevant to educational adequacy. As a result, to honor separation of powers (Buszin, 2012–2013; Umpstead, 2007), state courts decline to hear cases that challenge educational adequacy.

Paradox, next, materializes when state courts do accept a case that challenges adequacy. During a trial, "Adequacy courts must identify the level of quality that this [educational] system must exhibit" (Umpstead, 2007, p. 289). Educational adequacy becomes a paradox at this point because it is invoked as "a legal theory that calls for the provision of a *high minimum quality* education to all of the students in a state" (emphasis added) (Umpstead, 2007, p. 285).

This oxymoron, high minimum quality, is conventional wisdom about educational adequacy. A legal definition, thus, trumps a simple, necessary, but unexplored question: How can educational adequacy and *high minimum quality* be the same?

EDUCATIONAL ADEQUACY: A DEAD END

If something is adequate, it is generally defined as being of satisfactory quality. Educational adequacy, however, is set forth as a level of satisfactory quality—high minimum quality—that is as puzzling as it is indefensible. Evoked during court proceedings, educational adequacy is "defined as a level of resources or inputs that is sufficient to meet defined or absolute, rather than relative, output standards, such as a minimum passing score on a state achievement test" (Umpstead, 2007, p. 282).

Gaps between funding levels provided to different school districts, for instance, can be the basis for court challenges to educational adequacy (Hunter, 2018). But a dead end appears when conventional wisdom (funding is an input intended to yield an absolute output) is applied to concern like this about inadequacy. This dead end speaks to a question that conveys the inadequacies of conventional wisdom: What is the funding level that delivers a *high minimum quality* of education to all students as represented in standardized test scores?

There is no basis in educational research or practice for claiming that a known level of inputs results in absolute outputs for all students. There is no absolute level of outcomes from standardized testing, for example, that result from identified inputs for all students.

Conventional wisdom about educational adequacy as high minimum quality is pulled out of thin air. Expecting high minimum quality, as if this is a construct associated with the convergence of defined levels of inputs that yield absolute outputs, is the equivalent of expecting a tweet to explicate fully the nature of Truth.

Can Conventional Wisdom Be More Than Minimums?

Answering any question about educational adequacy with a response about high minimum quality suggests the extent to which students are shortchanged by, and the degree to which litigants fight an uphill battle with, conventional wisdom. Educational adequacy, even in the relatively friendly confines of state courts, comes to naught on the rocky shores of minimums masquerading as satisfactory quality.

Left to interpretation, high minimum quality is a phrase that adds little clarity to attempts to define, implement, and measure an adequate education for all US students. The impact of this conventional wisdom ensures that even when a court reaches a finding of educational inadequacy, the likely aftermath is protracted legal wrangling with no measurable improvement of adequacy in teaching and learning (Umpstead, 2007).

RECONSIDERING EDUCATIONAL ADEQUACY

Conventional wisdom is like an old hat; it's comfortable, fits just right, and never—from the point of view of the wearer—goes out of style. Conventional wisdom is the presumption that nothing is better than something that's "old hat."

With high minimum quality resting comfortably on the brow of American schooling, educational adequacy is a fashion statement about the lowest common denominator rationalizations worn by public education. Determining educational adequacy as high minimum quality implies that lowest common denominator teaching and learning establish satisfactory quality. Trapped by minimums, US public education is stuck with an especially useless old hat: linearity.

Conventional Wisdom and Linearity

The failure of constitutional provisions, court findings, and educational policy to prod policymakers and politicians beyond the paradox of high minimum quality serving as educational adequacy galvanizes linearity to

US public education. Linearity provokes misdirection throughout perceptions, decisions, and practices about educational adequacy.

Scholars of organizational theory offer a reference that illustrates the linearity that afflicts thinking about educational adequacy in the form of the I-P-O, or classic systems, model (Ilgen, Hollenbeck, Johnson, and Jundt, 2005). In the classic systems model, "Inputs lead to processes that in turn lead to outcomes (the input-processes-output, or I-P-O model)" (Ilgen et al., 2005, p. 519).

The bookends of linearity in the I-P-O model—inputs (I) and outputs (O)—dominate the study of and perceptions about relationships that yield minimum quality. As Ilgen et al. (2005) note, a purely linear model is not effective for understanding complex dynamics. Among other things, American public education is an extremely complex dynamic and linearity fails to take educational adequacy beyond minimums for several reasons.

First, linear models do not account for feedback within systems and, thus, do not incorporate feedback loops. Next, process within a linear model is a meaningless descriptor, an inert placeholder for the complexities between inputs and outputs in any system (Ilgen et al., 2005). Linearity, further, is a form of external control over educational adequacy. The manipulation of inputs and outputs, via policy for example, to measure minimum quality fails to account for the capacities of all students because it denies the "maximums" inherent in the complexities when education *leads-out*.

Mediational Influence

The presumption of linearity obstructs the realities, the art and the science, and complexities of public education. Limiting educational adequacy to the rigidity of input-to-output affixes minimums throughout public education. Linearity rivets high minimum quality to the blinders of singularity. The result is that contemporary declarations about a good school tend to be self-fulfilling prophecies that equate adequacy or purpose of public education with self-interest (Roda and Wells, 2013). Conventional wisdom, thus, becomes self-serving.

To unravel the self-interest that holds public education in place, this search turns to what Ilgen et al. (2005) refer to as *mediational influences* between inputs and outputs. Mediational influences can eliminate the minimums and linearity that forestall educational adequacy. The mediational influence identified for this search to attain educational adequacy unfettered by linearity is *throughput* (Swensson, Ellis, and Shaffer, 2019b).

In other disciplines, *throughput* is understood as the amount of materials that pass through a given system or process. In terms of this discussion, however, throughput is not material but is a teacher's classroom amalgam of cognitive, emotional, and behavioral engagement within the original power of education. Throughput, thus, is the interweaving of instructional behaviors (guided by educational function) to engage all students in the intersection of *how to think* and moral obligation.

Throughput is the responsive capacity within dynamic instruction. Throughput is the agency of pedagogy (*input-throughput-output-input*) applied in pursuit of engagement with satisfactory quality for all students. Deconstructing the barrier represented by conventional wisdom, inadequacy, and linearity can occur if public education is fueled by models and constructs and practices riveted to a transformed purpose for teaching and learning.

Inputs and outputs are necessary but not sufficient to the development of educational adequacy for all students throughout K–12 education in the twenty-first century. Public education can knock down the barrier of conventional wisdom with throughput serving as a battering ram. The effect of nonlinear mediational influence that expands professional practice—as this discussion will illustrate shortly—is to raise instruction and measurement beyond conventional wisdom throughout comprehensive public education.

SIX
The Measurement Barrier in US Public Education

Measurement, the evaluation of student academic proficiency, is an educational necessity. Measurement is power in education; as researchers observe, "Educational practice is driven by what we measure" (Cohen et al., 2009, p. 196). Two general types of measurement allow educators to choose and/or improve educational practice and, in turn, *lead-out* knowledge and cognitive processes of all students.

Formative evaluation (e.g., questions asked in class by teachers, homework, classroom quizzes, various class assignments/projects) and summative evaluation (e.g., final exams, end-of-unit assessments, culminating projects) assess the effect of instruction, the extent of growth of knowledge and cognitive processing of students, and guide ensuing instructional choices.

Hypothetically, measurement serves as a barometer. Data from this barometer is used by teachers to anticipate, guide, calculate, and respond to student academic performance.

In practice, however, assessment in contemporary public education is more barrier than heuristic. Measurement is a wall of numbers that policymakers, politicians, and others use to obstruct anything other than high minimum quality. Measurement imposes conventional wisdom—inputs, process, and outcomes (I-P-O)—upon US public education.

I-P-O AND MEASUREMENT: STANDARDIZED TESTING

Standardized tests solidify the barrier created by contemporary educational measurement. The towering presence of these assessments and the impact made by their numbers in US public education is overwhelming.

Standardized testing galvanizes conventional wisdom and the linearity of input-to-output to public schools. As a result, the role of classroom instruction deteriorates, classroom assessments follow suit, and the low-level academic expectations of standardized achievement tests abound (Barnum, 2018a).

The desultory purpose of contemporary public education and the attendant inadequacies and disparities visited upon urban students, students of color, rural students, and students in poverty position measurement as an inordinately negative factor in public education. A nightmarish educational scenario develops: standardized testing is responsible for "narrowing the curriculum in many high schools towards an almost exclusive emphasis in language and mathematics" (Reimers, 2006, p. 279).

Making matters worse, Heafner and Fitchett (2015) observe that "diverse and economically disadvantaged students are more likely to experience substandard classroom practices" (p. 230). This is high minimum quality pedagogy that assumes less academic aptitude among students of color (deficit thinking), responds to the lower-order cognition embedded in standardized tests, incorporates few opportunities for engagement with content, and limits cognitive pursuit of authentic texts in upper-level courses.

Measurement that does not elevate the adequacy of teaching and learning is a barrier that should not be. The purpose of this chapter is to examine the misnomers of measurement that obstruct educational adequacy throughout US public education.

MEASUREMENT AND ITS MISNOMERS

Educational measurement should inform educators about the extent to which student academic proficiency has been engaged with, and improved by, what has been taught. Both formative and summative evaluation in the classroom provide this feedback.

Standardized testing, by comparison, fossilizes measurement. As if encased in amber, the numbers from standardized tests share information about teaching and learning that is largely irrelevant. Regardless of when they are given during the school year, standardized test results report outcomes that have only a tangential relationship with student cognition. These results have little effect on instruction. Standardized testing wraps contemporary public education in the academic sediment of the past.

Nevertheless, proponents celebrate these tests and their outcomes because they constitute the building blocks of minimums in public education: accountability, efficiency, and cost abatement. These labels are measurement's misnomers. Debunking these misnomers is necessary if effective evaluation is to play a part in the transformation of educational adequacy for all US students.

Measurement Misnamed: Accountability

Measurement misnamed as accountability delimits public education. Standardized testing is the cudgel of accountability. The limitations imposed when measurement is misnamed as accountability are driven by the "basic logic of the system, which is that the thing that will drive school improvement is pushing people to improve test scores" (Barnum, 2018b; Garza and Garza, 2010). The ballyhooed linkage between measurement and accountability is so pervasive that "these tests operate as a form of control over classroom practices and learning" (Au, 2010, p. 2).

The claim that once-a-year measurement (standardized testing) renders accountability fails to account for the essential understanding that "all education measurement is an imperfect approximation to characterizing some properties of what is learned" (Reimers, 2006, p. 280). Deriving accountability for any aspect of teaching and learning based on the administration of one test is, at least, an incomplete judgment and, at worst, an improper claim "about what students know or how that changes over time" (Reimers, 2006, p. 280).

Scholars refer to "test prep" (Barnum, 2018b) as the instructional response to standardized tests overflowing with multiple choice and short-answer questions. Accountability incentivizes what will be referred to in this discussion as *knee-jerk pedagogy*. This reactive instruction is a self-defense tactic that prepares students for "predictable patterns in the test" (Barnum, 2018a).

When educators adopt and adapt this minimum quality instruction in response to accountability, a ripple effect rolls through schools and school districts. Several studies indicate that "high-stakes accountability for test score gains in reading and math can create competition between departments, thwart teachers from spending time collaborating with colleagues, and replace site-based management with increased district control" (Tichnor-Wagner, Harrison, and Cohen-Vogel, 2016, p. 609).

Research suggests that the multiple lower-order requirements of standardized testing do "students a disservice, as these kinds of exams are less likely to foster thinking critically and applying knowledge and further do not appear to even promote acquisition and retention of factual information to the extent stimulated by higher-order exams" (Jensen et al., 2014, p. 319).

In addition, as Sternberg and Grigorenko (2004) illustrate, contemporary measurement tends to evaluate analytic intelligence. As a result, "Children with creative and practical abilities, who are almost never taught or assessed in a way that matches their pattern of abilities, may be at a disadvantage in course after course, year after year" (Sternberg and Grigorenko, 2004, p. 278).

Under these circumstances, measurement is about piling up numbers of "right" and "wrong" answers as if these piles assess student thinking and as if they measure satisfactory quality. As researchers indicate, "High-stakes standardized testing promotes and encourages the deficit-thinking practice of 'teaching the basics'" (Garza and Garza, 2010, p. 202).

Public education's contemporary purpose—placing student cogs in the nation's economic machine—sustains the value assigned to accountability generated through predictability of measurement of lower-order cognition. Standardized testing results rivet public education to practices and skills intended that teach students to be better test takers. Accountability does little to guide or improve teaching to advance student thinking.

Avid misguided devotion to accountability traps teaching and learning in a cycle of lower-order cognition and the delimitation of student intelligences. Ironically, research indicates that test results—the numbers that signify accountability and judgment about the quality of educators and schools—have little positive effect (Patrick and Mantzicopoulos, 2016) on any aspect of public education. Scholars, meanwhile, lament that inflation of standardized tests scores is the most likely "measure" of the impact of accountability and efficiency (Barnum, 2018b).

Accountability tallies the extent of a student's aggregation of lower-order cognition in partial fulfillment of the contemporary purpose of public education (Reimers, 2006). Doubling back on itself, accountability measures only test-taking prowess and becomes the route to an educational cul-de-sac where both teaching and learning lead nowhere. Standardized testing abides; measurement stifles teaching and learning to assess low-hanging cognitive fruit, and minimums are, again, confirmed as educational adequacy.

Measurement Misnamed: Efficiency

Not only is accountability a misnomer for measurement, but also accountability is labeled with its own misnomer: efficiency. The assumption that pervades contemporary US education is that accountability is the source of school efficiency and that school efficiency is tantamount to educational adequacy. The twists and turns embedded in this misnomer are largely a product of legislative intervention and have little to do with satisfactory quality in teaching and learning for all US students.

Naming Rights: The Convenience of Efficiency

The contentious and confusing realm of public education appears to be an inconvenience for state legislators. The magnitude of this inconvenience is suggested by the fact that funding for public education often consumes half of a state's total budget. The ideological manipulations and financial disputes that accompany these dollars intrude upon projects and priorities to which legislators would rather devote their time and authority (Swensson and Ellis, 2016).

Moreover, meeting constitutional requirements for public education presents another inconvenience: *the public* expects educational adequacy from the efforts of lawmakers. Demands for satisfactory quality can be overwhelming.

Efficiency becomes the misnomer for measurement when a convenient response to demands for adequacy is required. Efficiency is a claim that legislators, politicians, and policymakers make as they exercise authority over the measurement of public education. Reducing the complexity of teaching and learning to efficiency allows legislatures to impose accountability conveniently while promoting beliefs that public schooling is too expensive and US education is in crisis.

Yearning for convenience, almost one-fourth of the state legislators in the United States are members of the American Legislative Exchange Council (ALEC). ALEC supplies its members with prepackaged model bills designed to establish efficiency and accountability throughout public education. ALEC members need only "fill in the blanks" of these legislative templates to create state-specific versions of measurement tied to free market ideology.

ALEC and a host of other organizations (Granger, 2008; Swensson, Ellis, and Shaffer, 2019a) promote and fund efforts to install efficiencies—increased class size, mechanisms of free market schooling, the elimination of teacher certification requirements—that reduce cost and lower taxes. Policymakers experience the self-justifying power of the synergy of struggle when efficiency is fostered. Efficiency is affirmed as measurement of "right" practices, answers, and mandates for public education.

Measurement Misnamed: Cost Abatement

Cost abatement assumes that low cost is a viable objective, a definition unto itself, for measurement. This assumption is that measurement as cost abatement (e.g., mass-produced, online, and computer-graded standardized testing) yields readily understood numbers (e.g., test scores for students, statistical manipulation of scores to assess schools/school districts, letter grades "awarded" to schools based on arbitrarily assigned ranges of scores) that evaluate educational adequacy. Efficiency and cost abatement go hand in hand.

The assumption that cost abatement yields measurement for public education is alive and well in the implementation of virtual schools and drill-and-kill computer-assisted learning. Cost abatement is proffered to measure satisfactory quality in contemporary public education.

THE FOG OF CERTAINTY

Accountability, efficiency, and cost abatement represent a little-discussed attribute of contemporary measurement. The use of standardized testing shrouds measurement in what will be referred to here as the *fog of certainty*. Akin to the self-serving justification known as my-side bias (Molden and Higgins, 2012), the fog of certainty is an absolute conviction about the "either" and "right" of a premise in education despite there being no basis in fact, data, or research for that conviction.

The fog of certainty hides the imprecision of standardized testing as it surrounds the use of these assessments with justifications that have nothing to do with *how to think* or the moral obligation of public education. The fog of certainty ensures "a vision of education that values highly what can be measured, and more problematically, it values most highly the measurement itself" (Gunzenhauser, 2003, p. 54). The fog of certainty wafts out of standardized testing when adult-centric outcomes are preferred from US public education.

Testing Bait and Switch

Standardized testing is heralded as a meaningful, extensive assessment of what students know. Yet proclaiming meaningful measurement where cognitive expression is limited to lower-order cognition and formulaic writing is the essence of bait and switch (Barnum, 2018b).

The effect of bait and switch in contemporary measurement is a prevalent feature of assessment employed to confirm "right" of an ideology. For example, PISA, the international assessment of reading, math, and science, offers itself as bait and is advertised by the Organisation for Economic Co-Operation and Development (OECD; the economic organization that administers it) as a test of "skills [that] are deemed to be essential for future life" (Sjoberg, 2012, p. 3).

Under the cover of the fog of certainty, the switch that occurs is particularly nefarious because data from PISA is used to recommend free-market policy and maneuver national education systems into alignment with the ideological perspective of OECD (Sjoberg, 2012). The bait, analysis of this test information to bolster students and their futures, disappears once the switch is made.

Proponents of privatization claim that the exercise of school choice — via mechanisms that give parents/caregivers the power to meet student needs — is school quality (DeAngelis and Erickson, 2018). These assertions of school quality imply strong testing results without data to support the claim. Thus obscured, measurement of growth in, or improvement of, student thinking is impossible to detect (Barnum, 2018b), and educational adequacy is switched in favor of choice.

Just More Numbers in the Wall

Statistical manipulations are undertaken to indicate that standardized testing results are valid and reliable. But these manipulations and their statistical surety generate measurement from student responses to extremely small numbers of questions about selected academic standards. Thus anchored, standardized testing results are offered as if they indicate the extent to which a school or school district is good.

The numbers and letter grades that convey measurement to parents and caregivers do have an impact. Studies find that "parental satisfaction positively correlates with a school's grade on its accountability report card (Charbonneau and Van Ryzin, 2012)" (Jacobsen, Snyder, and Saultz, 2014, p. 6). But numbers and letter grades associated with standardized testing do little more than build a wall that separates educational "winners" and "losers," with the result that parents/caregivers, students, and public schools are enveloped in fog.

Students Lost in the Fog

When accountability is the fog of certainty that descends on a "losing" school or district, educators are incentivized to implement test prep, to teach to the lowest common denominator, and to limit learning to those topics, subjects, or standards "covered" within standardized tests.

"Losing" schools and school districts respond to the fog of certainty with knee-jerk pedagogy. In addition, districts opt for instructional calendars to regulate a curriculum so it's devoted to test alignment. School districts may limit which students can enroll in courses at the middle and high school level and/or mandate attendance at "test prep" classes after school or on weekends (Tichnor-Wagner, Harrison, and Cohen-Vogel, 2016, p. 612). The fog of certainty forces educators to devote "inordinate time with concern about students' scores and not enough to student's learning" (Gunzenhauser, 2003, p. 56).

Scholars question the historic origin of standardized testing and the bias embedded in establishing test validity based on White student respondents only (Rector-Aranda, 2016). Moreover, scholars point out that the nation's allegiance to standardized testing creates *subtraction* in the school experiences of students of color when this fixation on standardized testing eliminates or reduces meaningful teacher-student relationships and stimulating engagement with academics (Rodriguez, 2008).

MEASUREMENT AND THE ILLUSION CALLED GAP-GAZING

Measurement in US public education succumbs to the illusion that observers call *gap-gazing* (Bonner, 2014). Gap-gazing is a fixation on the differences between standardized test scores earned by student cohorts.

Student cohorts (e.g., race, gender, free/reduced lunch, special education) are groups within any student body whose aggregate test performance is calculated and, then, compared with scores earned by other cohorts.

The illusion produced here is that although gap-gazing appears to engage educators with a focus on all learners, the reality is that the gaps have little to do with measuring or improving the cognitive capacities of all students.

Perseverating on the gaps between test scores earned by student cohorts, public educators are lured into a pernicious trap. Individual students fall between the gaps when educators assume that numbers about cohorts represent all learners in the cohort. In some cases, gap-gazing can serve the preconceptions of adults whose deficit thinking assumes a school-detached status for students of color or students in poverty. In other cases, gap-gazing pushes aside a focus on *how to think* and the moral obligation of public education in favor of test prep.

Gap-gazing, in one sense, prompts a reversal of the old saying about not being able to see the forest for the trees. Dividing the results of standardized testing into numbers that identify various cohorts of students was intended to ensure that testing progress was made by all students in all classes. The dilemma, however, is that clustering students by race, socioeconomic status, special education involvement, and/or gender took too many educators' attention away from the academic progress of each individual student.

The Weakness of the Bricks in This Barrier

Policy, ideology, and practice associated with measurement and its misnomers in contemporary public education erode teaching and learning (Strike, 2008). Others point to different effects where "bad test prep is test prep that is designed to raise scores on the particular test rather than give kids the underlying knowledge and skills that the test is supposed to capture" (Barnum, 2018a).

Standardized testing is a dull, imprecise instrument for measuring the interplay of habits of mind within the infinite and growing connections between axons and dendrites in the human brain. As one critic of standardized testing illustrates, "At the core of the new reforms is a commitment to a pedagogy of stupidity and repression that is geared toward memorization, conformity, passivity, and high stakes testing" (Giroux, 2014, p. 354).

Others note that inflation of standardized test scores across the nation confounds equity as one of the alleged goals of mandatory testing because inflated achievement test numbers facilitate "creating the illusion of improved equity" (Barnum, 2018a).

THE CASE FOR EFFECTIVE EVALUATION

Gap-gazing is symptomatic of the divide between measurement and what will be referred to during this discussion as *effective evaluation*. Students and educators have ample cognitive capabilities to take meaning-making well beyond the limited "ask" made about cognition in standardized testing. But the troubling divide between what is possible in cognitive terms and what is required by measurement is rarely acknowledged.

Effective evaluation is assessment of a student's academic proficiency in the intersection of *how to think* and moral obligation. Effective evaluation generates feedback that fuels instructional responses to sustain and increase student engagement with higher-order cognition (synthesizing, evaluating, creating).

Effective evaluation discovers what students have learned, based on what has been taught, so that this discovery can be used by educators to respond to students with further instruction devoted to remediation, enrichment, and/or new learning. Effective evaluation—absent the shoddy veneer of standardized testing—is the opportunity that US educators must use to disassemble the measurement barrier.

Examples of Effective Evaluation

Evaluation of student cognitive performance that is aligned with what's taught is often referred to as backward design (Wiggins and McTighe, 2005). This intensive connection between instruction and evaluation begins when teachers identify learning objectives during planning so that subsequent teaching engages students with the information and cognitive process required to fulfill the identified objectives (Jensen et al., 2014).

A rubric represents a practical example of effective evaluation. For the purposes of this discussion, a rubric would be composed of five vertical columns before instruction occurs. In this example, the far-left column conveys the lowest or most incomplete extent of learning a student can demonstrate regarding the subject, topic, or skill for which the rubric is written. The far-right column in this rubric establishes the most complete extent of learning expected from a student demonstration of the subject, topic, or skill for which the rubric is written.

Standardized testing represents measurement that seeks student responses that are the equivalent of the far-left column of this rubric. Seeking the least complete cognitive behaviors from students, and judging schools based on these, ensures that educators spend instructional time geared to meet the rock-bottom accountability and efficiency spawned by standardized testing. Instruction hits bottom when it focuses on remediation of student test-taking skills so that students who were not successful previously can rise above the expected minimum score.

Teaching to Cognitive Expectations

The capacity of human beings for meaning-making and the capability of education to *lead-out* meaning-making give effective evaluation its power. Effective evaluation—both formative and summative—engages students with demonstrations of improvement and growth of habits of mind. The cognitive behaviors expressed in these demonstrations—evincing knowledge and/or cognitive process that was shared during direct instruction and subsequent classroom engagement—are threads in the overall fabric of learning *how to think*.

Cognitive expectations explored during lessons or units of study constitute the feedback sought from students through effective evaluation. Research suggests several instructional behaviors that enhance the exchange in the original power of education and promote student engagement with these expectations during effective evaluation:

- *Persistent review* in the classroom—invoking what has been learned previously as a part of lessons devoted to new habits of mind or new problems—grows student learning through application and recycling (Bonner, 2014; Fisher and Frey, 2016).
- *Connections* between habits of mind and application of multiple thinking skills among multiple points of view and possible solutions. Evaluation and dialogue with students about evaluation expectations is one example of teaching that puts memory in position to recover knowledge and cognitive processes automatically.
- *Teachers' beliefs* about students are a key factor in resilience; how teachers demonstrate positive regard for the capacities of students promotes resilience in learners. Studies indicate that educators must embody resilience as a factor associated with student school success (Rodriguez, 2008; Samel, Sondergeld, Fischer, and Patterson, 2011).
- *Trusting relationships* established by educators with students have a positive impact on student academic outcomes and "one-on-one attention from teachers and consistent support from a specific adult had a positive effect on high school completion rates" (Samel et al., 2011, p. 98).
- *In combination*, when assessment and what will be referred to as *dynamic instruction*—a cognitive "ask" of students that requires the application of higher-order cognition to deal with a question, problem, or unknown—are unified, robust student outcomes ensue. Jensen et al. (2014) report, for instance, that "students who routinely took quizzes and unit exams requiring higher-order thinking not only showed deeper conceptual understanding by higher scores on

high-level questions, but also showed greater retention of the facts" (p. 317).

THE END OF MEASUREMENT INADEQUACY

Contemporary US education is confused about measurement. Measurement is undertaken to make education more efficient, less costly, and more accountable instead of serving to inform the improvement of teaching and learning.

This confusion extends into instruction. Confusion swirls throughout (1) instructional content, (2) the organization of this content to "fit" the knowledge demanded by testing, and (3) the instructional behaviors adopted to align with test expectations as educators attempt to meet the requirements that attend standardized testing (Au, 2010). Standardized tests lead instruction astray and replace higher-order cognition with lowest common denominator cognitive expectations.

How accountability results for schools and school districts are presented (e.g., letter grades, numbers) highlights the ultimate failure of America's intense focus on standardized testing. Studies indicate that the format used to highlight testing results, not the intellectual vacuum embedded in the results, "had the most significant impact on the perceived quality of the strong school" (Jacobsen, Snyder, and Saultz, 2014, p. 15). Confusion about the role of measurement is perpetuated by format, the mirage of the meaning of measurement.

Although time, effort, media attention, political wrangling, and ideological posturing are devoted to finding educational adequacy in testing—only to find that testing numbers are weakly associated with thinking—US public schools and educators are judged by numbers built on a house of cards. Moreover, research clearly indicates that standardized assessments put US students in a dismal cognitive place (Barnum, 2018b).

Measurement and instruction have a symbiotic feedback relationship. In this relationship, instruction (what is taught) is what gets tested (assessment), and assessment informs what gets taught next. In the age of assessment, however, this relationship is turned on its head.

Contemporary measurement becomes what gets taught and, in consequence, US public education turns 180 degrees away from dynamic instruction and effective evaluation. Instruction and what gets taught next are the same: bargain basement cognition. Moreover, one-and-done annual standardized assessments multiply the time, effort, and insight wasted in gap-gazing.

Ending the inadequacy of measurement demands acknowledgment of the shortcomings of standardized assessments. The inadequacy of instruction aligned with these shortcomings needs to be called out. The addiction to standardized testing as meaningful evaluation for teaching and learning encases US education in stasis.

SEVEN
Power and Public Education

Deconstructing the barriers that obstruct educational adequacy and the good public school is one thing. It's another thing entirely to move past the rubble of inadequacy to explore the determinants of comprehensive public education. When brought to bear, these determinants outline the public school that all US students deserve during the remainder of the twenty-first century.

The purpose of this chapter is to explore the first of these determinants: the relationship between education and power. This search suggests that this is a relationship fraught with imbalance. Competing powers and abuses of power symbolize this imbalance and the concomitant power failure of contemporary education. An examination of *the original power of education* begins this chapter and invites the restoration of balance required for comprehensive public education.

THE PRESENCE OF POWER IN EDUCATION

How education ensures that students are *qualified* for a productive adulthood, *socialized* to meet the expectations of society, and "subjectified" for new pathways throughout life illustrates overarching effects of what this discussion will refer to as *the original power of education* (Biesta, 2009). The original power of education that ensures qualification, socialization, and "subjectification" for all students is the exchange among intelligences during teaching and learning.

This exchange occurs during classroom construction of the intersection of *how to think* and the moral obligation of public education. Teaching and learning, when brought together under conditions necessary and sufficient for comprehensive public education, manifest this power.

Teaching is understood throughout this discussion as the power to *lead-out* student intelligences with knowledge, cognitive process, and/or skills beyond their personal assets. This power—which later will be referred to as *dynamic instruction*—engages students with accessing, acquiring, and accommodating knowledge, cognitive process, *how to think*, and the qualities of the moral obligation of public education.

This part of the exchange in the original power of education elicits community. Teaching draws out community because "the means of rationality norms, and criteria of appraisal, are themselves cultural artifacts invented by human beings and acquired from other human beings" (Strike, 2008, p. 120). Strike (2008) argues convincingly that mastering an academic discipline as a practice is an initiation into a community.

The other half of the exchange that is the original power of education, learning, is the power for meaning-making, natural thinking, and the multiple capacities of individuals including lived experience. These are the individual's assets of valorization. For the purposes of this discussion, *learning* is the student's power of cognitive ownership. The primary purpose of comprehensive public education (*how to think*), in consort with teaching, facilitates this ownership accessed, acquired, and accommodated as independent thinking.

Appropriating the community crafted in the exchange in the intersection of *how to think* and the moral obligation of public education endows each student with the capacity for principled reasoning. Reasoning and traditional public school's come-one-come-all enrollment illustrate why "it's important to have public schools play a role in helping young people and the broader community develop the capacity and commitment to live together in productive ways" (Mehta and Finnegan, 2019).

Unimpeded, the original power of education is the critical mass formed by teaching and learning as an exchange among and between intelligences. The original power of education has the potential to undo the desultory purpose and free market theorizing that plague contemporary public education (Swensson, Ellis, and Shaffer, 2019a).

THE RATIONALE FOR THE FUTURE OF US PUBLIC EDUCATION

The logical basis for the course of action that is the future for US public education—comprehensive public education—is built from the premise that the original power of education engenders independent thinking and that independent thinking is the bedrock for community in public education that fosters principled reasoning. Constructing knowledge in this way begins with instruction that puts students into authentic learning experiences designed to reflect upon habits of mind, norms, and values to make sense of their experiences in the world (Snarey and Samuelson, 2008, p. 54).

Principled reasoning is the fuel for this reflection, and it furthers valorization of lived experience, enrichment of the broad array of human intelligences, engagement with the values of moral obligation, and strengthening of "I identify as . . ." statements. Agency, the behaviors that ensue when principled reasoning is applied, develops in community via dynamic instruction in the intersection of primary purpose and moral obligation in the form of what will be referred to here as *freedom vis-à-vis learning*.

Freedom vis-à-vis learning is a student's self-regulation that does "not attach any sense of superior value to his cultural, ethnic, or racial identity but would instead see himself as a compound of several contingencies that make up the identity he had (Hill, 2000, 121)" (Reimers, 2006, p. 283). Freedom vis-à-vis learning is cognitive, behavioral, and emotional engagement with critical habits of mind that strike the balance found in the social contract and in the dynamic insight that "identity may be comprehensive without being all-encompassing" (Fraser-Burgess, 2012, p. 485).

Freedom vis-à-vis learning is necessary and sufficient for what Fraser-Burgess (2012) calls *positive liberty*, the "freedom to be ruled by the dictates of one's own reason" (p. 487). The worth of positive liberty and the rationale for comprehensive public education are magnified by research that indicates "that there are multiple identity profiles—some of which are individual and some of which are dual in focus—which predict different educational outcomes" (Worrell, 2014, p. 342).

These insights allow comprehensive public education to speak the power of positive liberty to honor the "I identify as . . ." statements of all students as the salient means to fulfill its moral obligation. Universality emerges when the exchange between teaching and learning fosters a student's capacity for self-regulation to perceive that all others deserve this same freedom.

To bring the original power of education, a primary purpose, moral obligation, and freedom into US public education during the remainder of the twenty-first century means that the exchange between teaching and learning must incorporate the "I identify as . . ." statements of all students into the rationale that supports and justifies the original power of education.

The Heart of the Good Public School

Unadorned by policy, politics, or ideology and undisturbed by contention, the original power of education is a dialectic between teaching and learning. As this exchange occurs, a synthesis of cognitive, behavioral, and emotional engagement emerges in the form of new knowledge and cognitive process for students. How the original power of education is expressed, and to what end, is the heart of the good public school.

Although transformative when unimpeded, the original power of education vies with two competing powers: *external power* and *internal power*. External power—expressed through politics, funding, policy, community mores, and/or the controversy du jour—vies with and often overrides the original power of teaching and learning. Internal power—disputation, disagreement, and disconnection among and between perspectives and publics of US public education—misdirects teaching and learning. Competing powers overlap and the original power of education short-circuits.

POWER: ABUSE AND POTENTIAL OF A STEADY STATE

The original power of education is a steady state. In other words, this power is always available and remains as it is defined in this discussion regardless of how it is applied and no matter the purpose for which it is employed. This means that the original power of education presents society with a double-edged sword. The sword that cuts both ways in US education is its purpose.

On the one hand, the purpose to which this steady state is applied carries with it the potential to foster freedom, universality, *how to think*, and principled reasoning. On the other hand, a pursuit of a different purpose is an abuse of this power when it is applied to aid and abet the timeless tendency of human beings to subordinate one another.

The dysfunction of the major perspectives; the myopia inherent in the synergy of struggle; the traffic jam of entities exercising political, financial, and legislative prerogatives; and the domination asserted by the power of privilege are all examples of factors and forces arrayed to abuse the original power of education. Uncritical habits of mind create conditions (including policy, statute, and practice) that foster discrimination and exclusion.

When Power Is Exclusionary

The contemporary purpose of education and the contemporary understanding of educational adequacy facilitate exclusion. Teaching is excluded from the vibrant range of intellectual and creative discourse by the narrow-mindedness of purpose and measurement. Students are excluded from independent thinking and positive liberty by mandates, statutes, and policies that impose minimum quality and survival of the fittest. Cohorts of students are subordinated when the original power of education is abused.

These exclusionary effects are an echo of subordination throughout US history between and among dominant and dominance-seeking racial, religious, ethnic, ideological, and socioeconomic groups. Historically, exclusion is endemic in the experiences of what scholars refer to as "involuntary minorities in the U.S. [including] American Indians, Alaska Natives, African Americans, Native Hawaiians, Puerto Ricans, and Mexican Americans" (Worrell, 2014, p. 337).

All experiences of individuals in these minorities are subject to "the dominant group [which] does not allow them the option of becoming equal members of the society" (Worrell, 2014, p. 337). The original power of education is frequently shanghaied to exclude and to dominate to the point that US students experience education in name only.

When this steady state is directed to exclude and discriminate, power overrides valorization, the moral obligation of public education, dynamic instruction, and the dialectic between teaching and learning. Domination is unleashed on behalf of separation and in justification of singularity.

US public education, under these conditions, can offer only minimum power to teaching and learning for principled reasoning and, as this discussion reveals, any minimum connotes the failure of educational adequacy. Minimums, for example, are visited upon schooling for the children of migrant farm workers whose first language is not English.

These students experience teaching and learning decimated by inadequate or nonexistent funding support. Neglect of education for the existing language skills of these students and neglect of the growth of their second language skills illustrates how abuse of the original power of public education denies the True North journeys of uncountable children.

THE MINOR LEAGUES: PURPOSE, POWER, AND EDUCATION

The contemporary purpose of public education establishes America's schools as the minor leagues of business and industry. Fueled by the external power of politics, this purpose frequently is summarized as *workforce development*. Workforce development identifies and targets entry-level employment as the focus of teaching and learning. Both federal and state lawmakers set their sights on fulfilling the contemporary purpose of public education via the implementation of workforce development.

The power behind the job-preparation purpose for public education is represented by the attempt at the federal level to combine the departments of education and workforce development. This potential marriage was justified as the way "to better evaluate 'how education and workforce development programs lead to successful labor market outcomes'" (Leonor, 2018).

At the state level, legislatures mandate workforce development as a priority for public educators, a misdirection at best. In Indiana, for example, public educators are required to earn professional growth points to renew their professional licenses. Added to existing requirements is that educators must devote time to develop partnerships and participate in what the legislation calls *externships* during which businesses provide the training.

The misdirection inherent in this latest mandate is that all teachers who renew their licenses must receive this training, including preschool and elementary educators. The fifteen points that must be earned via this new requirement constitute nearly 20 percent of the overall point total for license renewal. The legislature's effort to ensure that educators are "workforce friendly" not only steals time that otherwise could be used to explore a myriad of research-based instructional topics but also restricts the time available for training about local policy.

Educators must devote time to develop, then undertake, this training to earn professional growth points. The time to do this drains the original power of education when educators' energies are directed elsewhere.

Tunnel vision develops when job preparation replaces *how to think*. Because change is a persistent factor in any profession, skill, trade, or job, and given the necessity for "reinvention" throughout any career, riveting contemporary public education to workforce development restricts the range and depth of habits of mind that students will need during their change-infused employment futures.

Moreover, when power is applied from outside and inside public education to the exclusive advantage of either workforce development or STEM, emphasis is placed on preparation for only 7 percent of jobs in the United States (Fayer, Lacey, and Watson, 2017). Power that sustains the contemporary purpose of public education reinforces the minimums of educational adequacy.

WHY THE ORIGINAL POWER OF EDUCATION IS VULNERABLE

The original power of education is vulnerable. The impact of the collision between external/internal powers and the original power of education tends to foster absolutes—for example, TEO, the synergy of struggle, "right" and "wrong"—where the art and science of teaching and learning ought to be. The acquisitive frenzy to overwhelm and/or control the original power of education is represented in the efforts of proponents of the free market of schooling.

Amorality and External Power

The imposition of free market schooling (e.g., privatization, charter schools) devastates the original power of education. *How to think* and the moral obligation of public education are overwhelmed and a power unique to the free market appears: amorality (Lubienski, 2013). Without a moral sense, purveyors of free market schooling ridicule the original power of education by proclaiming that "modern policies become captive to the unwavering push for 'equality' at the expense of bona fide excellence, as demonstrated by the declining proficiency standards in public school tests" (Eng, 2013, p. 280).

Amorality in American schooling becomes one of many "collective problems which members of the subordinate group find difficult if not impossible to solve within the existing system of majority-minority relations" (Ogbu, 2004, p. 4). Amorality is only one instance of the willingness to separate and acquire an ideological "right" in public education that is one hundred and eighty degrees removed from the intersection of *how to think* and moral obligation.

The Many Effects When Wires Cross

The imposition of segregation in US schools, the use of statutory power to siphon funding away from public education, the denial of enrollment in publicly funded schools based on race, income, religion, or ethnicity—all are among the community-destroying effects when the steady state of the original power of education is purposed to serve ideological imperatives.

Policy and politics short-circuited the original power of education; for instance, when the No Child Left Behind Act 2000 (NCLB) was promulgated. NCLB was built upon the expectation that all students would earn a proficient standardized test score by 2014. A heap of unfunded implementation, remediation, and reporting requirements fell on educators over and above the time commitments required to administer the NCLB-mandated standardized testing.

Added to the avalanche of administrivia and lost instructional time, the standards upon which NCLB testing was based were subject to almost constant revision across the fifty states. A national effort to align test standards across all states, known at the time as Common Core State Standards, was rocked when several states opted out. A pervasive state of confusion arose about standards for testing that permeated what was to be taught, what was to be assessed, and how test results were to be used to help students.

Critical scholarship describes this situation succinctly where "education is not the great equalizer but a maintenance strategy in social reproduction" (Bourdieu, 1982; Garza and Garza, 2010, p. 203).

THE "WHAT," "WHO," AND "WHY" OF POWER IN EDUCATION

The promises made to all students in the foundational documents of public education go unfulfilled when manifestations of external power intrude. Internal power, moreover, misdirects the exchange that fuels teaching and learning in the intersection of *how to think* and moral obligation. Instead of securing the original power of education at its apex, contemporary US public education throws teaching and learning off balance. The "What," "Who," and "Why" of comprehensive public education lend a three-dimensional perspective to the need for a primary purpose in public education for the remainder of this century.

The "What" of Power in Public Education

The exchange in the intersection of *how to think* and the moral obligation of public education constitutes the "What" of power for comprehensive public education. "What" empowers all learners to give "consent regarding the treatment, rights, and well-being of others, which involves knowledge and skills imparted in public schools where children interact closely with those similar to and different from themselves" (Stitzlein, 2015, p. 576).

The "What" of comprehensive public education happens within "the free sharing of information [that] also creates the possibility of pedagogy—in which adults impart information by telling and showing, and children trust and use this information with confidence" (Mercer, 2013, p. 151). Understanding the "What" that all students deserve in public schools allows this search to gravitate toward the concepts, research, and data-based practices relevant to the primary purpose for comprehensive public education.

"What" develops differently, of course, when the original power of education is abused. Mechanisms, and other hokum bandied about as educational quick fixes, are the "What" forced upon contemporary US public education. Instead of the exchange within teaching and learning that enriches and extends student capacities, mechanisms exercise power that excludes and discriminates.

The "Who" of Power in Public Education

Students are the "Who" of power in comprehensive public education. The capacity to accommodate, acquire, and access knowledge and cognitive process in the academic context of classrooms and school environments is student power personified (Adams et al., 2016).

Examples of this power abound. The characteristics that successful learners in inner city schools bring with them including self-respect, command of Standard English, goal-setting ability, self-motivation, time management skills, consequence awareness, and respect for others represent the capacity and power of students (Hampton, 2016, pp. 425–26). The "Who" of power in education develops when habits of mind like resilience are "something that can be promoted by focusing on 'alterable' factors that can affect an individual's success in school (Benard, 1993)" (Hampton, 2016, pp. 426–27).

Asserting that all students have the capacities required to engage in the exchange of the original power of education is the research base from which comprehensive public education draws its clarity. As an example, multiple studies indicate that "black students' positive educational goals were backed up by their reported educational efforts, and in these inquiries the academic efforts were comparable among black and white students from similar socioeconomic backgrounds and/or in similar academic courses" (Diamond and Huguley, 2014, p. 772).

"Who" develops differently, of course, when the original power of education is abused. The adult-centric advantages fostered through policy, politics, and funding across contemporary US public education bypass students in favor of self-serving ideologies. The "Who" in contemporary US education are politicians, plutocrats, and pundits dedicated to their own goals on behalf of themselves.

When the "Who" of public education is adult-centric, self-interest and singularity are fostered. This state of affairs means that the potential for free, universal, and "public" in US education succumbs to the foundations and networks symbolized by neoliberal ideologies espoused by ALEC (Shaffer, Ellis, and Swensson, 2018).

The "Why" of Power in Public Education

To understand "Why" of the power of comprehensive public education requires acknowledgment that the original power of education is a steady state.

The original power of education, after all, is applied to transform capabilities, knowledge, cognitive process, skills, agency, and intelligences. The original power of education is applied to engage students with cognitive process, skills, knowledge, morality, citizenship, and life capacities. Controlling the "Why" of the original power, the steady state, of education has been coveted throughout history. To assert that an altruistic exercise of this control occurs throughout history, however, would be foolish.

"Why" develops differently, of course, when the original power of education is corrupted. Governments, ideologies, religions, political movements, and an endless assortment of factions and points of view throughout history have manipulated or usurped the original power of education. Instead of a student-centric exercise of the original power of education, the corruption of "Why" in contemporary education facilitates a disconnection from primary purpose and moral obligation in favor of efficiency, cost abatement, segregation, and marginalization.

POWER AND "I IDENTIFY AS . . ." STATEMENTS

Instead of proscribed and restricted manifestations of teaching and learning, the original power of education derives from understanding "that human intelligence is essentially social and cultural, and that the relationship between social activity and individual thinking underpins cognitive development" (Mercer, 2013, p. 153). Ensuring that the original power of education fulfills this relationship for all US students means that comprehensive public education must invest in *"I identify as . . ." statements*.

"I identify as . . ." statements are an individual's expression of lived experience, cognition, morality, and aspiration. These statements are an individual's most complete developing expression of self. The freedom emerging from the original power of education in comprehensive public education depends upon valorization of all "I identify as . . ." statements (Swensson, Ellis, and Shaffer, 2019b).

"I Identify as . . ." Statements

Freedom emerges when the original power of education engages all students with learning experiences that develop the capacity for independent thinking, principled reasoning, and positive liberty. These attributes developed in the intersection of *how to think* and the moral obligation of public education constitute the agency students can bring to their lives. This is agency required to live up to Eleanor Roosevelt's time-honored observation that "no one can make you feel inferior without your consent" (Roosevelt, 1937).

Any attempt to impose the feeling that Roosevelt in the mid-twentieth-century termed *inferiority*—today's understanding of subordination, discrimination, racism, marginalization—is absolute corruption of the power of the steady state and is exercised with no moral, legal, or ethical justification. Unjustified, immoral, or hate-filled denial of an individual's "I identify as . . ." statement must be challenged, and the gist of the challenge must arise from the critical habits of mind accessed, acquired, and applied by each student.

Roosevelt's statement speaks to the value of equipping all students with the capacities of principled reasoning for the ethical wherewithal to challenge threats to, or attacks upon, "I identify as . . ." statements. The intersection of *how to think* and the moral obligation of public education is the forum where this power is acquired so that no student consents (literally, figuratively, knowingly, or unknowingly) to hate, threats, or marginalization.

Cognitive, emotional, and behavioral agency put students in position to validate their feelings, foster the social contract, valorize their lived experience, and engage with others of good will. The original power of education grows students' capacities to defend against the intents, messages, and behaviors of people, policies, or practices that force inferiority upon any student's cognitive ownership and "I identify as . . ." statements.

"I identify as . . ." Statements and Stereotype Threat

A person's "I identify as . . ." statement is self-identity and how an individual valorizes. To illustrate the necessity for reconnecting US public schools with the original power of education so that independent thinking, principled reasoning, and positive liberty suffuse learning experiences for all students, a problem that students face daily deserves to be examined: *stereotype threat*. Stereotype threat is an emotional reaction that occurs when individuals "believe that their performance is being judged by others who have [a] stereotype in mind" (Worrell, 2014, p. 339).

Stereotype threat is the imposition of social influence to inflict self-doubt/denial. Those who invoke this influence do so to impugn or belittle some characteristic of a person's "I identify as . . ." statement. Stereotype threat occurs when someone conveys that another person's "I identify as . . ." statement is valueless, "wrong," unworthy, and/or beneath the "I identify as . . ." statement of the person holding the threat.

Stereotype threat is an assault on lived experience and the capacity for the power of learning. Stereotype threat is painfully obvious to anyone subjected to it and subordinated by it. Stereotype threat corrupts the original power of education when adults and/or schools evince this marginalization. When this happens, educators—including those who are silent about corruption despite working with others who do—unravel the care and trust required in a community devoted to the pursuit of primary purpose.

AVOIDING THE ABSOLUTES: POWER + CORRUPTION

Meaning-making and freedom vis-à-vis learning form a baseline for the power to be ruled by the dictates of one's reason. Drawn out by public education, this power grows in the intersection of primary purpose and moral obligation to effect the interaction of critical habits of mind within principled reasoning. Independent thinking, principled reasoning, and positive liberty allow "I identify as . . ." statements to flourish in a community where all students are accepted and encouraged.

Where there is power, however, corruption is not far behind. In the case of education, Lord Acton's maxim—"Power tends to corrupt and absolute power corrupts absolutely" (Acton, n.d.)—is confirmed when external power and internal power circumvent the original power of education. Instead of the exchange between teaching and learning, the original power of education is corrupted by uncritical habits of mind.

Uncritical Habits of Mind: A Case Example

The power of uncritical habits of mind to corrupt the original power of education is illustrated in the prevalence of the tyranny of either/or (TEO), the synergy of struggle, and stereotype threat. Reveling in "right" and denigrating "wrong" while identifying these as "either" and "or," uncritical habits of mind suppress the original power of education and wreak a devastating impact on *collective identity*.

Collective identity, as Ogbu (2004) indicates, "refers to people's sense of who they are, their 'we-feeling' or 'belonging'" (p. 3). In the late twentieth century, when this we-feeling first embraced pride in being Black, "a new public and psychological acknowledgement [in] the expression of Black collective identity" reached across all segments of Black America (Ogbu, 2004, p. 18). This expression of belonging and pride was met, however, in contemporary US society and education with an uncritical habit of mind: subordination.

Subordination is both the denigration of collective identity and the abrogation of educators' responsibilities to fulfill the promises, power, and moral obligation of public education in the lives and learning of all students. Subordination is TEO and the synergy of struggle invoked via uncritical habits of mind to identify "wrong" and to separate it as "or." Subordination of students of color is experienced as denial of and discrimination toward "I identify as . . ." statements.

Subordination within Contemporary Education

In response to pride in collective identity, a subordination narrative arose among some majority educators, pundits, politicians, and plutocrats. The expression of pride encompassed within collective identity was interpreted as resistance among Black students to education. Collective identity and pride were identified as "or." Collective identity and pride were subordinated as supposedly demonstrating opposition among African American students to academic achievement because it was the equivalent of "acting White" (Ogbu, 2004),

FREEDOM: THE ORIGINAL POWER OF EDUCATION

The original power of education is inaccessible in too many classrooms and schools. Until external and internal powers, and the marginalization, subordination, dysfunctional purpose, and educational inadequacy they produce, are supplanted, the original power of education cannot develop freedom for all students. Contemporary US education, its woebegone purpose, and its minimums manifest nothing less than singularity.

The exchange between teaching and learning engages students with capacities to choose the public good: the same rights and freedoms due all individuals. When students learn independent thinking, principled reasoning, and positive liberty, the primary purpose of comprehensive public education becomes a resource for all. The power of this resource lies in its application: individuals have the right to the reciprocity of freedom in fulfillment of the social contract.

This resource supplies the power necessary and sufficient for individuals to honor the freedom of others that all deserve for the greater good of community. From the original power of education, students acquire the capacity to refuse to give others permission to foster dis-identification via stereotype threat or marginalization. This is freedom in being governed by one's own reasoning balanced with choosing the public good. This power of universal principled reasoning is essential to the reconfiguration of educational adequacy in comprehensive public education.

Power for the Freedom of the Intentional Self

The original power of education to establish the reciprocity within individual's freedoms is at the center of the intentions and implications of comprehensive public education. This search confirms that (1) the original power of education derives from the fact that "'all knowledge is constructed' (Noddings, 1995, p. 115)" (Snarey and Samuelson, 2008, p. 55), and (2) freedom can be constructed by the original power of education.

The primary purpose of public education espoused throughout this discussion engenders the individual power of independent thinking, positive liberty, and self-regulation. Although the innumerable conceptualizations of self are topics for another discussion, what scholars refer to as *the intentional self* (Lapsley, 2008) encapsulates the freedom pursued in the good public school.

The intentional self encompasses an increase in an individual's "sense of being in charge, of being capable and responsible, a master of one's domain" (Lapsley, 2008, p. 36). This aspect of agency and its relationship with teaching and learning is identified as self-regulation or self-mastery. Self-regulation symbolizes the conjunction between moral obligation and *how to think* from which students acquire "access to socially valuable practices and their own voices within these practices as an agent of transformation of these practices" (Matusov and Smith, 2012, p. 291).

The intentional self is the power to balance and engage all individuals to "care about the sort of person we are, and we take steps to manage and control our behavior, motives, characteristics, and desires accordingly" (Lapsley, 2008, p. 35). The power of comprehensive public education is, of course, not the only factor relevant to the self, *how to think*, and moral behavior, or the lack of it. But comprehensive public education has the power to play a pivotal role in the many ways that *how to think* and morality incorporate as positive liberty within personality (Lapsley, 2008).

Ending the struggle over "right" and "wrong" in US public education means the balance of power found in a balance of "goods" is possible in the conjunction of student assets with *leading-out* by public education. Curtailing all the forces and factors that anchor contemporary public education to stasis is within reach of the original power of education if primary purpose and educational adequacy are identified as the means to reach this objective. The means to this end (another of the determinants that can engage all students with freedom vis-à-vis learning and the reciprocity of freedom within the social contract) lies within the grasp of every educator in every one of America's public schools: *dynamic instruction*.

EIGHT

Dynamic Instruction

Act I—Function, Evaluation, Precursors

The original power of education is the potential of every traditional public school. The activation of this power and satisfactory quality in public education cannot be separated.

But the vulnerabilities of the original power of education ensure that educational adequacy for the good public school cannot develop unless several decisive factors are identified and acted upon. *Dynamic instruction* is one of these determinants.

Dynamic instruction—an educator's professional behaviors in a classroom's admixture of science, art, pedagogy, information, care, cognitive process, creativity, intellect, data, and emotion—*leads-out* the capacities of all students. Dynamic instruction releases the original power of education in a "pedagogical exchange as a form of value creation rather than knowledge transmission" (McWilliam, 2008, p. 266).

Making sense of the world is a persistent enterprise of the human brain. Dynamic instruction is the decisive means by which pedagogy validates, grows, and improves the meaning-making and moral centering of all students. Dynamic instruction is the facilitating professionalism that activates the exchange within the intersection of *how to think* and the moral obligation of public education. Empowering students with *how to think*, in schools where the moral obligation of public education is a daily practice, provides access to resiliency, persistence, and optimism (Hampton, 2016).

Dynamic instruction is the professional decision making and classroom agency that engages all students with principled reasoning so that "other cultural views are recognized as such and deliberation involves acknowledging the respective reasons of the various cultural views, then selecting the rules that establish fair terms of cooperation based on reconciling the evidence and reasons" (Fraser-Burgess, 2012, pp. 497–98).

Across the United States, however, the original power of education and dynamic instruction have limited influence in America's classrooms. Instead, stasis fostered by the contemporary purpose of public education, the debilitating impact of standardized testing, and the parasitic effects of free market theory enforce what amounts to the dumbing-down of instruction. "Teachers in low-performing schools were likely to change in ways less conducive to improving general instructional practices and more focused on improving data (i.e., focusing on testing skills rather than attempting to improve learning)" (Jacobsen, Snyder, and Saultz, 2014, p. 6).

The purpose of this chapter is to share the first of two acts in which dynamic instruction plays a leading role as a determinant (the interplay of constructs, pedagogy, ideas, and decisions that *activate* the original power of education) that directs a student-centric focus for the original power of education. The spotlight illuminates three characteristics of dynamic instruction—*educational function*, *effective evaluation*, and *instructional precursors*—at center stage in Act I.

SETTING THE STAGE FOR DYNAMIC INSTRUCTION

Before dynamic instruction can develop, educators must jettison popular but ineffective notions alive and well in contemporary instruction. Popularity obscures the negative impact that these notions have on the original power of teaching and learning. Teaching must transition out of ineffective instructional behaviors represented here by learning styles and the presumption of stable teaching.

Learning Styles Are Instructionally Anemic

The notion that individual learners exhibit a predominate learning style is so popular that this idea is conventional wisdom not only in education but also across society. This attempt to connect instruction with students is ubiquitous because it translates readily into classroom practice "since learning styles are premised on the notion that students who are taught using their preferred learning style will manifest stronger academic performance" (Worrell, 2014, p. 335).

When this notion is accepted, teaching is conducted as if it's a matter of matching instructional behaviors with learning styles. However, not only are there few experimental studies that investigate this notion, but those that undertake such an inquiry "do not support the hypothesis of improved achievement due to matched learning styles (Pashler et al., 2008; Rohrer and Pashler, 2012)" (Worrell, 2014, p. 335).

Stable Instruction Is an Unreliable Presumption

The multitude of choices made during instruction can originate from the cornucopia of research about knowledge and cognitive process for pedagogy. To incorporate this wealth of research-based strategies and methods while teaching, instruction must be nimble. Furthermore, when students respond during instruction, educators must select and apply the resources from this cornucopia relevant to the student(s) and the learning intended by the lesson.

Contemporary instruction, however, is tangled up in the notion that teaching must be a stable enterprise. Recipes or teach-by-numbers models expect and mandate (in the case of teacher evaluation) a lock-step implementation of instructional behaviors. Presuming that instruction is stable ignores the role that choice and response play in every lesson. What ought to be an exchange between intelligences too often becomes a learning desert, barren except for worksheets, repetition, and truncated cognition.

The presumption that instruction must be stable to be effective is not borne out by research. "There is very little empirical evidence to support assertions that teaching effectiveness is stable" (Patrick and Mantzicopoulos, 2016, p. 26).

Instead of assessing educator performance as if its quality is expressed via instructional stability, educator performance should be valued to the extent that it aligns with RTS (Return to Students) within the intersection of *how to think* and moral obligation. Understanding instruction and its effectiveness, in this light, means that a transformation of educational adequacy demands responsive, flexible, and dynamic instruction.

DYNAMIC INSTRUCTION

To transform educational adequacy and to identify the good public school while, at the same time, curtailing the circumstances responsible for the stagnation of instruction, public educators must turn to a talent that has served teachers from time immemorial: weaving.

This metaphor captures the warp and weft of expectations, concepts, knowledge, ideas, skills, responses, and cognitive process during classroom instruction. Dynamic instruction is the shuttle that weaves these "threads."

Dynamic instruction yields complex design and texture. Pedagogy is the ability of an educator to apply the original power of education in any classroom, for all students, and across subjects or grade levels. Dynamic instruction compensates for the vulnerability of the original power of education and for the disconnections between this power and pedagogy when educators create and apply *educational function*.

Educational Function

Educators craft educational function. Educational function is composed of "sets" of ideas, concepts, knowledge, strategies, assumptions, and outcomes compiled to orient dynamic instruction and to facilitate what will be referred to in this discussion as *instructional mapping*.

Sets are interconnected and multidirectional. Teachers (in grade levels, teams, subject areas, departments, schools, and/or school districts) take responsibility for evolving the array of sets in educational function. Sets establish a repository for a teacher's application of educational function in the choices made prior to, during, and after dynamic instruction. Sets also align with students' prior, and future, learning. Sets constitute the palette of pedagogical possibilities that implement the original power of education.

Educational function constitutes a kind of instructional GPS for the journey toward primary purpose in comprehensive public education (Swensson, Ellis, and Shaffer, 2019b).

How an educator uses this GPS to orient instructional choices and decisions is unique to the educator, to the lessons taught, and to the existing capacities and prior learning of students. Educational function orients a teacher's access to student engagement that lies in the fundamental understanding that "the child is an active interpreter of information and general experience" (Nucci, 2008, p. 291).

The original power of education is multifaceted and capable of engaging student capacities at the highest levels of cognition. Dynamic instruction expresses the interactive, reciprocal, sometimes dialectical, and always complex nature of this power. Educational function orients teachers as they craft the multidirectional and interactive nature of dynamic instruction (Swensson, Ellis, and Shaffer, 2019b). The complexity of teaching and learning is attended to with satisfactory quality when interweaving accesses a means for orienting and supporting throughput.

Educational Adequacy and Educational Function

Educational function holds the key to a transformed understanding of educational adequacy because educational function orients the pedagogy crafted during dynamic instruction. Educational function supports throughput and permits *formative substantiation* of adequacy. In turn, each student's expression of *how to think* supports the *summative substantiation* of educational adequacy.

When public educators attend to educational function, educational adequacy cannot terminate at high minimum quality because mediating influences incorporate feedback loops that give rise to continuous improvement. Educational function accounts for a range of professional variables and responses to student cognitive resources.

Educational Function and Instructional Mapping

When teachers connect the sets within educational function and make choices while teaching, throughput occurs and dynamic instruction is underway. *Instructional mapping* occurs during dynamic instruction when educators weave and interconnect sets, student responses, and objectives of the lesson to sustain and improve the pursuit of *how to think* and the moral obligation of public education. Instructional mapping endows dynamic instruction with the capacity to craft student engagement without relying on formulaic or lock-step teaching.

Pedagogy, educational function, and instructional mapping give any educator the capacity to weave dynamic instruction. Meaning-making and social construction are affected by the original power of education when dynamic instruction is common ground upon which the intersection of primary purpose and moral obligation are built.

Effective Evaluation

Effective evaluation calls forth the extent to which students can apply and articulate what has been taught. Habits of mind, knowledge, cognitive process, independent thinking, values of moral obligation, principled reasoning, and positive liberty explored during class illustrate the broad "content" of effective evaluation. One well-known example of effective evaluation is the Advanced Placement (AP) exam.

Every AP exam engages students with authentic challenges based on the cognitive processes and habits of mind explored in an AP class. For instance, relevant historical documents are sources students use to craft their answer to a concept-dense, open-ended question posed in an American History AP exam. Before the test, of course, students know neither the question nor the documents. Students do know, however, the community of concepts and habits of mind taught during class. AP exams exemplify effective evaluation because they are designed to assess the *how to think* taught throughout the school year.

Effective evaluation—whether formative or summative—empowers both teachers and students. For example, when educators set forth in advance what students are expected to learn during class, studies indicate this makes it more likely that students will learn successfully (Fisher and Frey, 2016).

Dynamic instruction cannot be separated from effective evaluation. Effective evaluation is part of what this discussion refers to as *a priori* pedagogy. Effective evaluation originates alongside a priori pedagogy in the robust planning made possible by educational function. Planning for each lesson or unit focuses on an amalgam of relevant sets from educational function to build an "eye on the prize" persistence in the choices and decisions at the heart of the original power of education. The professional behaviors of dynamic instruction incorporate this planning during the delivery of lesson objectives.

Jensen et al. (2014) suggest that when instructional expectations derived from a priori pedagogy incorporate learning higher order cognitive tasks via dynamic instruction to be assessed in class, students alter their study habits in anticipation of academically demanding measurement. These same researchers found that when assessments engaged students' higher order thinking, conceptual understandings at a deeper level occurred alongside strong fact retention.

Instructional Precursors

Most people have played one of the games during which the object is to remove portions of a tower without causing the structure to collapse. Inevitably, a piece is removed, gravity takes over, and the tower comes tumbling down. Although dynamic instruction is much more complicated than these simple games, if the right piece is missing, instruction also tends to collapse.

Instructional precursors are among the pieces of dynamic instruction that, when they aren't present, can bring teaching and learning crashing down.

Instructional precursors are an essential part of the cognitive foundation necessary for student engagement during dynamic instruction. Referred to as "ground rules" by some observers (Mercer, 2013, p. 160), instructional precursors are aspects of cognition, behavior, and emotion that students learn to augment their engagement during the exchange in the original power of education.

Instructional precursors put students in position during dynamic instruction to build upon prior learning and to create connections with new knowledge and habits of mind:

- "cognitive strategies of rehearsal, elaboration (through summarizing and paraphrasing), and organization" (Lee and Shute, 2010, p. 191);
- a focus on resiliency as a capacity of learners as noted in the work of "Solberg et al. (1998) [who] identified six key skills as the foundations of educational resiliency: building confidence, making connections, setting goals, managing stress, increasing well-being, and understanding motivation" (Hampton, 2016, p. 428);
- telling students what's expected before it's taught, engaging students to explain what they can do and how they can think while they learn what's being taught (Fisher and Frey, 2016);
- self-regulation strategies including "planning, skimming, and monitoring comprehension" (Lee and Shute, 2010, p. 192);

- "creative pedagogies [that] merge traditional academic content and popular culture, particularly in contexts serving Latina/o and other historically marginalized students" (Rodriguez, 2008, p. 263);
- research-based variables related to frameworks such as OTL (Opportunity to Learn) "defined as the degree to which a student is exposed to specific content, cognition, and pedagogical practices (Kurz, Elliott, Lemons, Zigmond, Kloo, and Kettler, 2014)" (Heafner and Fitchett, 2015, p. 229);
- modeling ideas, constructs, habits of mind, and other examples of cognitive agency during lessons to make "concepts accessible to the learners through structured, guided practice; encouraging reflective learning; increasing on-task behavior; and increasing student engagement and achievement (Brophy, 1986; Housand and Reis, 2008; Methe and Hintze, 2003; Sandholtz, 2011; VanDeWeghe, 2006; Watson and Bradley, 2009)" (Harbour et al., 2015, p. 7);
- talk-abouts conducted as an iteration of a priori pedagogy that puts dynamic instruction into position as a precursor unto itself by "demonstrating a desired skill or behavior while simultaneously describing the actions and decisions being made throughout the process (Archer and Hughes, 2011)" (Harbour et al., 2015, p. 6);
- talking students "through" habits of mind and sharing (out-loud, visually, etc.) connections between habits of mind while using language that draws out knowledge and cognition necessary to make the most of these connections during lessons, problems, concerns, or other authentic dilemmas;
- giving students frequent opportunities to "respond during instruction rather than passively listening, they had higher levels of achievement" (Harbour et al., 2015, p. 8); and
- providing feedback to students to facilitate their access to self-efficacy. Giving opportunities to respond fuels emotional engagement. Feedback constitutes a trifecta for instruction when it occurs alongside modeling and opportunities to respond. Feedback engages students in monitoring and adjusting how-to during learning.

Instructional precursors are cognitive tools that engage students with habits of mind, cognitive process, and knowledge that facilitate independent thinking. Precursors allow students to *lead-out* from what they know to what they have not known previously. Instructional precursors are yet another example of freedom that emerges from authentic learning experiences and dynamic instruction in the intersection of primary purpose and moral obligation.

Instructional precursors are strategies, processes, mnemonics, and jump-starts for cognition taught to give students initial independence to make meaning during dynamic instruction. Teaching precursors means that teachers supply cognitive short-cuts that students can access on their own when the original power of education goes to work on new knowledge, habits of mind, or cognitive process.

ACT I: EXEUNT ALL

Good public schools articulate "clear expectations, establish instructional coherence across classrooms, and provide consistent and constructive feedback to students (Jang et al., 2010)" (Adams et al., 2016, p. 172). These characteristics of effective evaluation inform each teacher about "next steps" that follow dynamic instruction based on what students have or have not yet learned.

Dynamic instruction engages all students in "mastering complex skills that can be performed outside the teacher's presence" (Fisher and Frey, 2016, p. 525). Authentic, applied, and active instruction intends to put students in position to interconnect habits of mind via the layers of their brains and develop the fabric of *how to think*. Examples of the threads of dynamic instruction shared here suggest not only the components and goals of instruction that pursue a primary purpose, but they also implicate the higher-order thinking that interdisciplinary teaching and learning entails.

> The evidence suggests that teachers who use student-centered instructional strategies, engage students in learning through non-controlling language, encourage choice in the selection of tasks and projects, and allow for independent thinking are more effective at developing motivated and engaged students. (Black and Deci, 2000; Hardre and Reeve, 2003; Reeve and Jang, 2006; Reeve et al., 2004; Soenens and Vansteenkiste, 2005) (Adams et al., 2016, p. 175)

Dynamic instruction is the convergence of educational function, primary purpose, and moral obligation supported by each educator's principled reasoning. Educational function orients the array of research, professional experience, caring, and pedagogy at the command of each teacher during dynamic instruction to establish the reciprocal and dialectic relationship at the center of the original power of education.

When educational function, effective evaluation, and instructional precursors take a bow at the conclusion of Act I, the stage in every public school classroom is set for teaching aligned with the original power of education. Teaching, however, is only 50 percent of this original power. The other half of the original power of education, learning, must be accounted for on stage. Act II of this brief presentation about dynamic instruction, as a result, shines a spotlight on the role that student engagement plays in comprehensive public education.

NINE
Dynamic Instruction

Act II — Student Engagement

The previous chapter put the spotlight on the roles played by educational function, effective evaluation, and instructional precursors during dynamic instruction. This chapter, Act II in the performance of dynamic instruction, brings student engagement to center stage. Instead of instruction serving as a delivery system that dumps lower-order cognition into the laps of passive learners, student engagement ensures that learning is maximized as the other half of the critical mass required to generate the original power of education.

The goal of this chapter is to explore student engagement. If educational adequacy is to become more than a minimum experience for all US students, student engagement must be given a starring role in dynamic instruction.

STUDENT ENGAGEMENT AND SATISFACTORY QUALITY

Every public educator knows that "teaching is enormously demanding, frequently frustrating, occasionally overwhelming, and always an eclectic mix of planned formality and spontaneous serendipity" (Campbell, 2008, p. 607). Educators also know that the original power of education develops from this mix when students are engaged during lessons.

Studies identify a host of instructional behaviors that foster engagement, including modeling, opportunities to respond, and feedback (Harbour et al., 2015). Active student engagement "can lead to greater gains in true conceptual understanding as well as greater retention in the STEM subjects" (Jensen et al., 2014, p. 308).

A reciprocal relationship is established when dynamic instruction and student engagement create an exchange of intelligences across multiple elements of the Taxonomy: "application, analysis, and evaluation encompass processes that benefit retention (memory)" (Jensen et al., 2014, p. 311). The fabric of learning woven during this exchange ensures that "long-term learning is not about recalling discrete facts but rather [about] mastering complex skills that can be performed outside the teacher's presence" (Fisher and Frey, 2016, p. 525).

The Triumvirate of Student Engagement

Dynamic instruction sparks a triumvirate of student engagement: emotional, behavioral, and cognitive. Active student participation in class exercises is *behavioral engagement* (Harbour et al., 2015). Dynamic instruction invests in behavioral engagement via authentic, problem-centered, active learning. Students engage with information and cognitive process to accommodate habits of mind capable of investigating, resolving, exploring, creating, and/or evaluating unknowns, concerns, issues, or conundrums.

Emotional engagement is the affective reaction of students to school adults and peers. Emotional engagement, also, is the overall reaction of students to school climate, culture, and environment, that influences "students' feelings of connectedness and identification with the school" (Harbour et al., 2015, p. 5).

Connectedness with school and learning depends on teacher interactions that foster emotional engagement. Emotional engagement takes on additional significance from research that suggests that dynamic instruction reflects the "complementary nature of classroom social and instructional climates (Durlak et al., 2011)" (Curby, Rimm-Kaufman, and Abry, 2013, p. 565).

Also, reflected in the complementary nature of these climates is the moral obligation of public education and the importance of valorizing all "I identify as . . ." statements. As Rector-Aranda (2016) reminds the profession, educators must know that "identities are something we 'do,' not that we are, and we can act these out, perform them, often unwittingly, in different ways in different situations" (Rector-Aranda, 2016, p. 12).

Cognitive engagement calls forth students' effort, investment, "and willingness to use complex learning strategies and processes needed to master and comprehend various ideas (Fredericks et al., 2004; Ladd and Dinella, 2009; Wang and Holcombe, 2010)" (Harbour et al., 2015, p. 5).

PEDAGOGICAL AGENCY

Where student engagement, the exchange of intelligences, and principled reasoning ought to flourish, the doldrums of high minimum quality and adult-centric policy prevail instead. Under the aegis of the contemporary purpose of education, the burden of educational inadequacy falls with notable savagery on "culturally diverse and economically disadvantaged students [who] are more likely to experience substandard classroom practices" (Heafner and Fitchett, 2015, p. 230; Kozol, 1991).

Dire educational circumstances, however, can be surmounted if *pedagogical agency* is instituted via dynamic instruction to establish student engagement. For the purposes of this discussion, pedagogical agency is each teacher's focus "on forging relationships, tackling novel challenges and synthesizing 'big picture' scenarios" (McWilliam, 2008, p. 264).

The Expectations of Pedagogical Agency

Pedagogical agency is a professional disposition without which dynamic instruction falters. When they forge, tackle, and synthesize, public educators have no intention to anchor instruction with predetermined, one-size-fits-all, vendor remedies or canned strategies. Instead, the expectations of pedagogical agency are the impetus for dynamic instruction:

- *leading-out* what students bring to class (e.g., meaning-making, natural thinking, lived experience) into engagement with habits of mind or thinking skills.
- *making professional choices* that emphasize the "active nature of children's brains as they cognitively construct or organize structures of thought and action" (Snarey and Samuelson, 2008, p. 55).
- *developing active interpretation* that Strike (2008) refers to as human flourishing and personal development.

The expectations of pedagogical agency guarantee that dynamic instruction is the antithesis of stasis. Pedagogical agency drives novel challenges in the classroom during which it is not the case "that every student should love physics and Shakespeare, but that every student should encounter practices that develop a range of excellences and the capacity to experience a range of complex goods that develop capacity and transform experience" (Strike, 2008, p. 126).

Pedagogical agency in comprehensive public education is built upon *collective efficacy*, which is the degree "to which teachers as a group share the belief that they have the power and capability to help students learn, to control instructional practices, and ultimately to make a difference in student achievement (Bandura, 1997; Ware and Kitsantas, 2007)" (Lee and Shute, 2010, p. 195).

Authoritative Engagement

As the fuel for engagement in the exchange between intelligences, dynamic instruction engages all students with subject area disciplines and their practices (based on standards of excellence pursued ethically and norms associated with them), via "authentic instruction [which] views the current state of a practice as authoritative but not as authoritarian" (Strike, 2008, p. 124).

The range of choices, professional behaviors, and responses that occur during dynamic instruction are authoritative when the intersection of primary purpose and moral obligation exist as every educator's True North. As Honig and Coburn (2007) suggest, the rich interplay that represents authoritative practice can be encapsulated in three categories: sense-making, social construction, and response to ambiguity.

Sense-making is the agency required when educators determine meaning and what, if any, instructional choices align with meaning to craft student engagement. Decisions about meaning also put educators in position for social construction of the implications, and application, of this decision making. Together, sense-making and social construction are agencies with which educators can respond to ambiguity in the ideas, constructs, strategies, and/or research that form the building blocks of pedagogical agency and educational function within dynamic instruction (Honig and Coburn, 2007).

LANGUAGING AND STUDENT ENGAGEMENT

Student engagement depends on language. Languaging is the access point for educators to student engagement. The power of language and language acquisition is depicted when external language (teacher vocalizations, student comments, print materials, online language) becomes (after the fact, when the vocalization or printed language are memory) "'inner speech,' which is used in individual reasoning" (Mercer, 2013, p. 156).

Dynamic instruction, as a result, requires an intense investment in "languaging": conversing, reading, writing, speaking, listening, internalizing, and paraphrasing. Languaging is a form of modeling in the sense that educators choose language as an investment in orienting student engagement. Languaging provides students with a "how to" about habits of mind, knowledge, and/or cognitive process.

Languaging, scholars have argued, is an experience that affects "the development of the ability to self-regulate [and] could thus be a crucial, transformative feature of cognitive development" (Mercer, 2013, p. 156). The gist of languaging in dynamic instruction is the engagement of all students with accessing and accommodating "external" language from teaching into their own learned "internal" language.

The importance of language and language acquisition is highlighted by scholarship about *how to think* and its relevance as the primary purpose of comprehensive public education. When adults talk during lessons about their thinking as the thinking occurs, students gain a sense for the how-to of meaning-making shared in the teacher's cognitive interplay. This how-to becomes a student's new knowledge; languaging facilitates the dialectic in the original power of education to transform external teacher-talk into internal student-talk.

Languaging, in this sense, is modeling *how to think*. When educators choose languaging during dynamic instruction and make modeling or the explanation of the languaging part of this teaching, students can acquire internal languaging. Internal languaging becomes part of memory, which enables retrieval and facilitates independent, internal, application of this modeling.

It is important to emphasize that although languaging clearly involves verbalization, this dialogue also happens when internalization (the "inner voice" of cognition) interacts with the written word, and/or visuals, within textbooks, classroom activities, and/or relevant social media. The cognitive exchange between external and internal languaging—a primary example of the original power of education—is represented by the dialogue created during a think-aloud.

The Languaging of a Think-Aloud

Explicated by several scholars (Fisher and Frey, 2008; Mercer, 2013), a *think-aloud* is a teacher's verbalization-as-modeling of her/his cognitive choices and behaviors. Think-alouds occur when a teacher talks-through her thinking while modeling the how-to process of learning something. Think-alouds resemble an instructional monologue replete with questions, doubts, and observations that the teacher's self-talk employs while learning, for example, to comprehend a passage in a book, or to incorporate multiple points of view about a topic.

Students adapt and adopt the knowledge and cognitive process shared during a think-aloud. Languaging out loud and via "inner voice" engages students with learning and practicing to transition their cognition beyond formula-style answers (Mercer, 2013).

These representations illuminate "claims about how language-based collaborative learning and problem solving might shape individual learning and development" (Mercer, 2013, p. 155). The exchange in any dialogue oriented and structured by dynamic instruction intends to shape *how to think*, and this intention recognizes the relationship between languaging and memory.

The Relationship between Languaging and Memory

How to think is memory dependent. Various scholars indicate that "memory is the foundation for all other teaching because students cannot think critically (or any other way) about what they know if they do not know anything" (Brown, Roediger, and McDaniel, 2014; Fisher and Frey 2008; Sternberg, 2002, p. 386). The original Bloom's Taxonomy and its revision identify the essential role of memory as the foundation of *how to think* (Bloom, 1956; Krathwohl, 2002).

Memory is not only about recall of facts and information. Memory extends to automatizing thinking skills or habits of mind. Mnemonics, schemas, diagrams, and other visual representations of languaging and the recall of external languaging symbolize the tools students can access memory to engage with authentic learning and unknowns.

Sternberg (2002) discusses several habits of mind that engage students with memory learning, including *matching* items from one set with another, *recognizing* and *recalling* facts learned previously, and *verifying* the accuracy of statements/information based on facts recalled from memory (p. 386).

Student Engagement and Habits of Mind

Dynamic instruction honed by the modeling within languaging is a powerful factor for student engagement and achievement. "Modeling promotes increased student engagement and academic performance, resulting in collateral benefits such as increased use of self-regulated learning strategies and enhanced responses to higher order thinking questions and tasks (Housand and Reis, 2008)" (Harbour et al., 2015, p. 7). Under the influence of languaging, habits of mind are opened to behavioral, emotional, and/or cognitive engagement.

Habits of mind give educators a cognitive interface with students beyond natural thinking into the realms of analyzing, evaluating, and creating identified as higher-order cognition in the revision of Bloom's Taxonomy (Krathwohl, 2002). Habits of mind taught, learned, and utilized during authentic and active learning experiences shuttle back and forth through lessons to engage students in weaving *how to think* (Swensson, Ellis, and Shaffer, 2019a).

A Curtain Call for Act II

A curtain call to applaud the enduring value of student engagement via dynamic instruction acknowledges the roles played by "actors" essential to engagement:

- *Corrective feedback* supplies "specific information about what the student is doing incorrectly and needs to do instead [and] can im-

prove academic and behavioral performance (Hattie and Timperley, 2007)" (Harbour et al., 2015, p. 10).
- *Trust-filled relationships* between students and educators must be crafted and maintained because when students—especially students of color and students in poverty—have trust-filled relationships with educators, they are "metacognitively, motivationally, and behaviorally active learners. Such students act volitionally toward academic goals and possess the agency to control academic efforts (Reeve, Ryan, Deci, and Jang, 2008)" (Adams et al., 2016, p. 170).

Teaching that engages students in processes like listening to others, giving reasons for ideas shared in class, encouraging all members of a group to give input, taking notes that summarize each person's input, and/or reaching consensus about sharing with the class provides students with precursor skills for academic success (Mercer, 2013).

THE REVIEWS ARE IN: DYNAMIC INSTRUCTION

Dynamic instruction is neither recipe nor list. Rather, dynamic instruction is the amalgam of professional decisions and choices available to and made by a public educator to engage all students with active learning in pursuit of *how to think* and the moral obligation of public education. It is within the exchange in the original power of education that the capacities and intelligences of all students grow. Several assumptions underlie the student-centric foundation of dynamic instruction:

- The intersection of *how to think* and the moral obligation of public education is constructed by the original power of education.
- The original power of education is maximized in pedagogical agency. Pedagogical agency is unique to each educator; expandable and flexible, pedagogical agency can be shared. Pedagogical agency is inert, however, in the absence of an orientation supplied by the educator via educational function and without the instructional agency of student engagement.
- Dynamic instruction occurs when an educator plans, acts, and evaluates the behaviors and pedagogy required to engage all students in a lesson or unit of study.
- Dynamic instruction engages students in active learning experiences aligned with the primary purpose of public education.
- Dynamic instruction brings the original power of education full circle in the intersection of *how to think* and the moral obligation of public education. *How to think* is underway when students interweave habits of mind during authentic learning experiences. Habits of mind are applied (alongside existing knowledge, cognitive pro-

cess, and lived experience that students possess) to authentic problems, unknowns, and issues. Dynamic instruction is the fabric woven by educators to engage students with habits of mind that put them in position to weave positive liberty.
- Instructional mapping is a teacher's responses to students during class that advance the plan of a lesson. Instructional mapping describes the ongoing cognitive behaviors of recognition and response implemented in alignment with educational function and the objective of a lesson.

Comprehensive public education is the convergence of pedagogical agency, educational foundation, and dynamic instruction in the choices of each educator. When dynamic instruction yields the transformation of educational adequacy so that adequacy is measured by the understanding that "a student has only mastered something if she can do it when confronted with unfamiliar particulars" (Barnum, 2018b), common ground in comprehensive public education develops.

Common ground ensures a focus on the original power of education. The power exercised by each public educator during dynamic instruction engages all students in comprehensive public education. Alone, however, dynamic instruction constitutes only a parcel of the common ground required to transform teaching and learning. Policy is the next parcel that increases the breadth of educational adequacy and moves this search for the good public school forward.

TEN
Policy and Idiocy in US Public Education

Educational adequacy, the effectiveness of public educators, the quality of day-to-day teaching and learning—all are affected by policy. Policy is responsible for key elements in the contemporary purpose and minimal quality of America's education.

The future for US public education does not have to repeat the disconnections and denial imposed by contemporary policy. Dynamic instruction, the original power of education in US public schools, and comprehensive public education for the remainder of the twenty-first century will be available to transform teaching and learning on behalf of all US students if the decisive effect of policy is brought to bear.

A power unto itself, policy can build or destroy any aspect of public education. As this discussion reveals, however, contemporary policies that influence America's public schools are not designed for building or even for destruction. Instead, US public education policy fosters idiocy.

Au (2010) invokes the original Greek root of idiocy, *idios*, as a warning about the danger and damage that results when educational policy exalts individual goods at the expense of public goods. *Idios* means "private, self-centered, selfish, and separate" (Au, 2010, p. 8). In calling attention to the root of "idiocy," Au makes the essential observation that education in a democracy must teach *"against* idiocy" (emphasis original) (Au, 2010, p. 8). Educational policy ought to be subject to the same admonition.

Disastrously, educational policy and idiocy often are one in the same. Privatization and exclusion (the pinnacle of selfish educational policy) are nurtured by contemporary educational policy. Policy, in addition, separates. Policy that divides and excludes—fostered by ideology and politics—is the abrogation of the original power of education.

For the future, policymakers have a choice about US public education: engage with the intersection of *how to think* and moral obligation, or, be idiotic.

The purpose of this chapter, on the one hand, is to examine the ruinous influence of idiotic policy on contemporary public education. The purpose of this chapter, on the other hand, is to examine the potential of policy to transform how educational adequacy is understood. This search confirms that the mandates and whims of educational policy rarely attend to the common ground of dynamic instruction, moral obligation, or primary purpose. The goal of this chapter is to give direction to policy that contributes to community, universality, balance, and common ground in US public schools.

THE IDIOCY OF CONTEMPORARY EDUCATIONAL POLICY

Educational inadequacy is sustained in contemporary US public education by "the practices and policies adopted by schools and governing agencies" (Burch, 2007, p. 85). Feckless policymakers sustain stasis and inequity throughout contemporary US public education with policies that drain the original power of education and that erect barriers to the teaching and learning that all US students deserve. Idiocy in contemporary educational policy is manifest in the separate and self-centered presence of linearity, fantasy, and ignorance by choice.

The Idiocy of Policy: More Linearity

Self-interest and singularity are fostered by policy afflicted with the same linearity that dominates measurement and free market theory. Contemporary educational policy supports and advances a purpose that creates separation. Devoted to outcomes aligned with political and ideological imperatives, self-interest is ingrained in educational policy. Community, the original power of education, and universality are too complex and too associated with feedback to "fit" with linearity.

Federal policymakers, for example, proposed (near the end of the second decade of the twenty-first century) the singularity of "merging 'all of the existing' programs at the Education and Labor departments into a single new 'Department of Education and the Workforce,' or DEW" (Leonor, 2018).

This consolidation was rationalized as a means "to better evaluate 'how education and workforce development programs lead to successful labor market outcomes'" (Leonor, 2018). Nothing says linearity like outcomes galvanized to the contemporary, limited purpose of public education that is indifferent to, and seeks separation from, large segments of

US students. Linearity denies the value of feedback and sees only what is revealed in the mirror of self-interest.

Further evidence of the linearity of educational policy is found in Michigan. Michigan authorized the creation of public charter schools in 1993. Twenty years later, three hundred charter schools operated across Michigan. In 2011, a cap on the number of charters was eliminated by legislation. Separate and self-serving, over 80 percent of Michigan's charter schools are in the hands of for-profit businesses (Reckhow, Grossman, and Evans, 2015). Traditional public school systems in Muskegon Heights and Highland Park were turned over to operators of charter schools (Reckhow, Grossmann, and Evans, 2015, p. 214).

The linearity of policy that drives the wholesale privatization of Michigan's public schools separates most students from academic success. Academic achievement throughout Michigan is abysmal. Data gathered near the conclusion of the second decade of this century showed that Michigan's test scores were at the bottom nationally in terms of improvement of student academic proficiency and that 70 percent of the state's charter schools occupied the bottom half of overall state rankings (Swensson, Ellis, and Shaffer, 2019a).

The Idiocy of Policy: Fantasy

All parents and caregivers want what's best for their children. Consumer demand for quality in public education, scholars note, is a constant. But too much contemporary policy promotes the fantasy that separation and exclusion address this constant. The reality is that "public education does not respond to true market conditions" (Brown, 2002, p. 112). When policymakers pretend that privatization is a response to educational demands made by all parents/caregivers, families, and students, an epic fantasy is perpetrated.

Consumer demand is irrelevant, in the case of public education, because the market exists for the market's sake. This is the amorality of the marketplace (Lubienski, 2013) that, in terms of policy, is a manifestation not of response to consumer demand but of the idiocy embedded in self-interest represented by policy that nurtures accountability, fiscal efficiency, and cost abatement.

The fantasy that self-interest improves educational quality plays out when traditional public schools are so fiscally eviscerated that they are left with little recourse but to respond with "less qualified teachers, a higher student/teacher ratio, and fewer support services" (Brown, 2002, p. 112). Moreover, free market proponents promote the fantasy of ideological purity in policy where efficient, low-cost education is advanced in funding mechanisms masquerading as public education (Jacobsen, Snyder, and Saultz, 2014).

When mechanisms, like tax credits, are promoted, the story line of low-cost and less government induces *the public* to believe policy fantasies and arrive at misguided "perceptions because those taking advantage of tax credits often do not view themselves as direct beneficiaries of government support and programs (Campbell, 2011; Koch and Mettler, 2012; Mettler, 2007, 2011)" (Jacobsen, Snyder, and Saultz, 2014, p. 5).

The Idiocy of Policy: Ignorance by Choice

Policymakers, politicians, pundits, and plutocrats turn a blind eye to educational research because studies and data do not serve their policy interests. Educational policy mavens choose ignorance to the point that "research findings are not reflected in current educational policy" (Cohen et al., 2009, p. 187).

The reason that policymakers and ideologues choose ignorance and eschew data to direct educational policy is confirmed by studies that find that when research is applied for policymaking, the data tends to "remove politics and ideology from those decisions and other influences that may threaten efforts to focus central office decision making on teaching and learning (e.g., Coalition for Evidence-Based Policy, 2003; Slavin, 1989; U.S. Department of Education, 2002a)" (Honig and Coburn, 2007, p. 582).

Choosing ignorance, choosing to avoid research, insulates policymakers; data-free policy facilitates "right" decisions aligned with separate and self-serving ideologies. Choosing ignorance is easy, and this choice frees policymakers from dealing with the ambiguity associated with research (e.g., "which" research is relevant and how should relevant research be "used") (Honig and Coburn, 2007).

The choice to avoid research-based evidence allows policymakers and politicians to craft policy that ignores the copious data that illustrates the woeful academic results and market failure that speaks volumes about the educational disasters fostered by ignorance. Choosing ignorance is the idiocy of policy that undercuts the original power of education. Data-free policy is an ideological safety zone that, ironically, takes advantage of research that found "that policy decisions regarding data dissemination can have profound effects on public perception" (Jacobsen, Snyder, and Saultz, 2014, p. 17).

Contemporary educational policy relies on linearity to sustain fantasy that is data poor and *idios* rich. Why include data or research in educational policy when self-interest and separation are best served without it?

THE WRECK OF THE GOOD SHIP EDUCATIONAL POLICY

Contemporary educational policy is a vessel stranded on the rocks of self-interest. Educational policy is marooned because "politicians, community leaders and other stakeholders are frequently engaged in political battles that give rise to disjointed decisions" (Ikpa, 2016, p. 468). Worse, as in the case of measurement, educational policy continues to echo its historic ignorance reaching "back to the I.Q., eugenics, and scientific management movements in education of the early 1900's (Au, 2009b)" (Au, 2010, p. 2).

Without a focus on primary purpose and moral obligation, policy readily becomes the means to an end divorced from the original power of education. Ill informed and data-free, educational policy is created by policymakers drawn to the siren song of reform.

Policy and the Siren Song of "Reform"

In US education, the irresistible aura of a quick fix surrounds the word *reform*. Applying this term to US education and its policies, practices, proposals, and purposes attracts interest, funding, and advocacy. Because the supposition of panacea is a powerful force and because a siren song is not subject to reason, only infrequently is a simple question asked of those who are drawn to the siren song: *What is being reformed and how?*

For reform proponents, one answer to this question resonates: public education, by any means. But this fire-ready-aim approach to educational policy illustrates that reform frenzy yields a confusing and counterproductive array of fruitless outcomes:

- The volume of standards-based reforms far outstrips the capabilities of schools and their governing bodies to deal with this tsunami of change (Burch, 2007).
- Reform policies siphon millions in state funding away from traditional public schools (Swensson, Ellis, and Shaffer, 2019a).
- The products, programs, and practices sold to public education in the name of reform act "as carriers of broader cultural norms that frequently reinforce the very practices that reform designs aim to change" (Burch, 2007, p. 86).
- Policy fails students and misdirects education when it embraces reform for its own sake. This outcome is measured in the academic devastation generated when the tyranny of either/or imposes standardized achievement testing as "either" and "right."
- "There are at least 747 public charter schools around the country that enroll a higher percentage of white students than any of the traditional public schools in the school district where they are located" (Felton, 2018b, p. 7).

LOCALLY SOURCED POLICY

The imposition of policy that articulates a blind faith in reform constitutes further evidence that contemporary public education is ill equipped to transform educational adequacy in the learning experiences of all US students during the remainder of the twenty-first century.

Sustained inadequacy does not indicate, however, that policy is an ineffective resource or an unnecessary tool for the future of comprehensive public education in the United States. On the contrary, putting policy to work on behalf of comprehensive education has the potential to restore universality and refocus teaching and learning on the original power of education.

Fulfilling this potential depends on adapting the wisdom expressed in the time-honored observation that all politics are local. A corollary to this generalization is required to establish comprehensive public education: *all educational policy is local*.

Educational Policy: A Mutable Dialectic

The value of this corollary is illustrated when educational policy is employed locally as a mutable dialectic: (1) federal regulations and mandates depend on action by state and local entities to carry them out, and (2) "states and districts have at times established considerable independence from federal policymakers by evading or modifying policy to meet local needs (Berman and McLaughlin, 1977)" (Marsh and Wohlstetter, 2013, p. 277).

Policy, it turns out, is not linear if educators don't allow it to be. The interface between imposed policy and locally sourced policy constitutes a flexible zone where there is leeway for the student-centric purpose and moral obligation of comprehensive public education.

Practices and procedures engineered locally via policy in this zone put educators in position to nurture a compelling synthesis where *how to think*, the moral purpose of public education, dynamic instruction, effective evaluation, positive liberty, and independent thinking become the policy backbone of comprehensive public education.

A Snapshot of the Mutable Dialectic for Policy

This dialectic is already recognized as one resource for the transformation of US public education. As Burch (2007) observes, "Although policy designs and behavior are connected to larger social and cultural beliefs, these frames can change as people go about their work and as they implement policies and plans" (p. 84).

Such a transformation happened, for instance, when school districts employed waivers and various work-arounds to modify aspects of the

No Child Left Behind Act of 2001 (NCLB). "These concessions, as one scholar noted, demonstrated the 'political power of some districts and federal propensity to engage in bargaining during policy implementation' (Vergari, 2007, p. 331)" (Marsh and Wohlstetter, 2013, p. 278).

At the state level there are further examples of how "local" can transform policy. As the expectations and requirements of NCLB escalated over time to increase the pressure on states to meet stipulated targets for standardized test scores, "states receiving NCLB waivers have created ways to comply with federal policy intent while protecting their interests and authority" (Marsh and Wohlstetter, 2013, p. 278). The give and take represented in instances like these suggest the value of understanding the transformative role of locally sourced policy.

REMOVING IDIOCY FROM THE POLICY MENU

Transformation of the purpose and adequacy of US public education can be activated locally by coalitions of public school teachers, leaders, and school boards during collaborative local policymaking. Existing associations of these primary actors in public education occupy a strategic position for confederating theory and practice to design and carry out locally sourced policy.

The key to this initiative and the abiding value of locally sourced policy lies in understanding that "relations among federal, state, and local governments are bidirectional" (Marsh and Wohlstetter, 2013, p. 281).

Twenty-First-Century Educational Policy

To remove idiocy from the menu, several ideas explored during this search are food for thought for use of the dialectic in, and bidirectionality of, educational policy. Engaging with this approach at the local level can bring balance to public education via policy implementation:

- *The Local of Policy*. Because the contemporary adjudication of educational adequacy does not rise beyond minimums and because little of substance occurs in the wake of court decisions that determine inadequacy, local policies must leverage the implementation of comprehensive public education. Policy for comprehensive education in the twenty-first century is best crafted, first, at the local level (Buszin, 2012–2013):
  - Locally sourced policy is the power to offset mandates from state or federal authorities with strategic responses that focus on locally identified priorities (e.g., the intersection of *how to think* and moral obligation). Locally sourced policy also can

be used to manage compliance options (e.g., waivers, local work-arounds) that ensure student-centric educational adequacy.
- Locally sourced policy is a powerful tool for collaboration between teacher associations and school administration. The governing body of a public school district, of course, is the final authority for promulgating policy. But recommendations developed via collaboration among school district educators takes policy out of the realm of cookie-cutter originators (e.g., companies that develop policy drafts for a fee), beyond the self-serving influence of ideological originators (e.g., ALEC, foundations), and past the historic, often counterproductive, adversarial relationship between teachers and administrators.
- Locally originated policy provides an opportunity for beta testing in the educational "real world." Before final promulgation by the Board of Education, policy can be piloted and evaluated in terms of its alignment with local priorities. Taking advantage of research about professional practice, practitioners can select among abundant data and test the impact of proposed local policy on satisfactory quality for all students.
- Locally sourced policy can establish training about educational function to guide and orient teaching and professional practices.
- The importance of locally sourced policy is aligned with research that "increasingly suggests that teacher quality is a critical variable in predicting a child's academic achievement" (Buszin, 2012–2013, p. 1633).
- Further, locally sourced policy and well-trained, research-savvy educators have a profound advantage because the incorporation of data and research within dynamic instruction yields cognitive agency for all students (Honig and Coburn, 2007).
- Locally sourced policies can eliminate stasis; for instance, with stipulations for balancing staff assignments in all schools with master teachers so that the least experienced teachers are not relegated to the poorest schools or most difficult classrooms (Lee and Shute, 2010).

- *Policy for Measurement.* Regardless of how it is characterized—accountability, assessment, evaluation—measurement in contemporary public education is a policy cudgel tied to "performance data [that] hold many promises, including enabling citizens to more accurately judge their public institutions (Moynihan 2008)" (Jacobsen, Snyder, and Saultz, 2014, p. 2). But measurement imposed by con-

temporary policy does little to fulfill promises about freedom, universality, or improved academic performance.
   - Studies reveal that measurement enforced by the policy predisposition for standardized testing as measurement has little impact even on the minimums that pass for educational adequacy. Contemporary measurement fails to assess student cognition beyond "right" or "wrong."
- Effective evaluation determines the growth of a student's *how to think* with the result that dynamic instruction improves to create additional student growth. Locally sourced policy to this end can grow from simple expressions such as these:
   - The policy of this school district is to evaluate each student's *how to think*.
   - The policy of this school district is to develop formative evaluations that align with the primary purpose of comprehensive public education. These evaluations will be assessed for their effectiveness, and evaluation will be a subject of continuous improvement throughout the school district.
   - The policy of this school district is to share with parents, caregivers, and the community the primary purpose of comprehensive public education and how this purpose is measured to ensure the school and life success of all students.
   - The policy of this school district is to measure job performance by staff members using research-based, locally developed instruments and analysis that align with district-based policy and standards for RTS. Return to Students encapsulates the broad spectrum of objectives embedded within the professional performance expectations for all staff in this district. The improvement of performance to sustain and grow the intelligences of all students will be the purpose of staff evaluation and staff development conducted throughout this district.
- *A "Strengths" Point of View*. RTS (Return to Students) can be affected in policy through what researchers refer to as the "strengths perspective" (McMahon, Baete Kenyon, and Carter, 2013):
   - The policy of this district is to value the lived experience and other individual resources that students bring to school as viable and important resources for student engagement with *how to think*.
   - The policy of this district is to ensure that all students have access to professionals who enhance and expand their intelligences. In addition to outstanding teachers, these resources

include, but are not limited to, mental health/counseling support, social worker involvement, full-day nurse presence in school, and a comprehensive range of learning opportunities (e.g., the arts, technology education, vocational education, physical/health education, traditional subject area disciplines, foreign languages).
- It is the policy of this school district to establish partnerships with community agencies whose professional expertise permits the district to meet its policy goals of support, wellness, and healthy school environments for all students.

Simply put, a strengths approach to locally sourced policy places a premium on the assets that students, their families, and communities bring to public education. Policy that recognizes these strengths, and that lays the groundwork for educator training to maximize student strengths, augments the primary purpose and moral obligation of comprehensive public education. Policy that recognizes these strengths builds bridges between school and families.

- *Policy Feedback Theory.* The linearity of contemporary educational policy proceeds from the assumption that politics is an input or independent variable while policies are the output or independent variable (Jacobsen, Snyder, and Saultz, 2014). Policy feedback theory can be employed to end linearity in educational policy.

Policy feedback theory demonstrates that beliefs and perceptions of *the public* are influenced by policies. Once public attitudes are influenced, these revised beliefs function as feedback in a cycle that reenters "'the political system, shaping the political environment and the possibilities for future policy making' (Campbell 2008, 962)" (Jacobsen, Snyder, and Saultz, 2014, p. 5).

Using this theory as a foundation, educational policy becomes a transformation agent and a filter through which educators can access feedback about both locally sourced and externally mandated policy. Several topical areas present themselves for putting this cycle to work on behalf of *the public*'s affinity for comprehensive public education:

- *Perspectives and Publics.* Policy has the capacity to bring much needed improvement to the relationship among perspectives and publics. Instead of turning a blind eye to the innumerable conflicts and unavoidable misdirection that infest this relationship, future policy helps educators adopt a model that guides and improves the legal profession.

  A confederation of educational associations and school boards could create a shared authority for policy promulgation. Such a confederation might be called the "American Educators Association" (AEA), mirroring the confederation of State and National Bar Associations.

Instead of subjecting teaching and learning to the tyranny of either/or and the vagaries of ideologically infused mandates, this policy-generated collaborative could design, implement, grow, and assess educational policy. Policy in this vein would put a priority on student learning monitored and measured through professional collaboration and the exercise of educational function in pursuit of *how to think* and the fulfillment of the moral obligation of public education for all students.

- *Termination of TEO*. The TEO yields nothing of value in public education for US students. The proposed policy role for an AEA would entail the establishment and monitoring of policy to terminate tyranny of this kind. In the absence of TEO, policy could move toward common ground throughout US public education.
- *The Eye of the Student*. Contemporary policy linked to publics and perspectives of American education sustains a purpose that literally leaves students behind. The eye of the beholder looks backward. Little in contemporary policy serves as a guide for the future of public education in the United States.

Instead of the status quo, policy for comprehensive public education must be student-centric. Dynamic instruction, educational function, effective evaluation, moral obligation, and *how to think* become the student-centric baseline from which policy can be used to construct the expectations of and support for the good public school.

COMMON GROUND: POLICY FOR THE GOOD PUBLIC SCHOOL

Comprehensive public education requires policy to be the statement of expectations, future directions, and common ground on behalf of all students. Educational policy for the remainder of the twenty-first century must respond to the catastrophic effects of contemporary school policy. The future of US public education depends on a turn to locally sourced policy as the student-centric and bidirectional means for transformations that take advantage of research findings that confirm that:

> The way in which school choice policies are written, regulated, and implemented has huge implications for the kinds of outcomes they will foster, both in terms of their short-term effects on school-level racial diversity and their long-term effects on political support for public education. (Roda and Wells, 2013, p. 287)

Application of the research and constructs encountered thus far in this search suggests policy priorities that are the common ground necessary and sufficient for *21CPE*.

- *Valorizing all students*. Policy must jettison the current "hear no, see no, speak no" approach to race, culture, and poverty in public education. Building relationships with students' families and promoting the strengths of the cultures of the school-community deserve a place within school policy.

  Scholars indicate the power and importance of relationship-building because it entails the trust that permits dialogic communication (Bonner, 2014). Establishing a standard for the role of trust through communication in public education, policy can affect access for educators to cognitive behaviors, decisions, and actions that recognize and engage the individual capacities of all students.

- *Embracing the public good*. Numerous scholars indicate the debilitating effect of "free-market models of individualism and high-stakes competition" (Rector-Aranda, 2016, p. 1) and the atrophying of public good within American education. Policy to restore the public good can begin with understanding that "children in integrated schools are more likely to graduate high school and attend college, and they get jobs with higher incomes" (Mehta and Finnegan, 2019).

ELEVEN

Recovering the "public" of US Education

At one point in US history, "public" conveyed the *universal* and *free* intended by constitutional imperatives for education. Knight Abowitz (2011) suggests the scope of this intention in her observation that "a public is a group undergoing the consequences of a shared circumstance" (p. 476). Education that is universal and free appends the term *public* to convey a generalization about all citizens in America's democracy: they are "connected by common concerns about their shared fate, care for the interests of others, and the desire to seek shared principles that enable them to work out differences" (Stitzlein, 2015, p. 566).

Fundamental premises about "public" like these, however, are an uncertainty for contemporary US education. Clamorous and divisive relationships between and among perspectives and publics and misdirection of teaching and learning abandon "public." Sometimes despicable, often anemic, impulses from power, policy, and conventional wisdom invoke a Darwinian ethos so that only a limited number of "winners" emerge in America's schools.

Survival of the fittest in the educational marketplace mirrors the subtext of history where the absence of "public" is the norm for too many US students. Rife with examples of exclusion, discrimination, and oppression—including, but not limited to, Native American subjugation, slavery, denial of women's rights, WWII internment of Japanese Americans, discrimination against immigrants, and LGBTQ+ marginalization—America's history and US public education ride parallel tracks devoid of "public."

Although "public" remains elusive in too much of US education, this search suggests that envisioning educational adequacy as the wellspring of universality and freedom is key to fulfilling the promises of American education. This future, socialization guided by moral obligation from which the shared and consequential relationship of the group emerges, is "public" shaped by the transformation of the purpose of comprehensive public education. The goal of this chapter is to discuss "public" and the responsibility of educators to shape the intents of "public" into educational adequacy.

THE SHARED CIRCUMSTANCE OF "PUBLIC" IN EDUCATION

Once integral to the promises of American public education, "public" shakes atop the tectonic plates of self-interest, singularity, myopia, and survival of the fittest. Rattled, the sense of "public" associated with contemporary US public education is "now largely diffused, inchoate, unable to conceive and articulate forcefully an alternative, more genuinely democratic vision of educational reform" (Granger, 2008, p. 222).

As if policy, politics, perspectives, and practice did not generate enough dysfunction throughout contemporary US public education, many Americans are so disconnected from "public" that they perceive that the only good public school is one "that will affirm their own social, political, and, increasingly, even religious worldviews" (Stitzlein, 2015, p. 565). Common purpose and "public" in US education tremble along the fault lines of the tyranny of either/or, the synergy of struggle, and the minimums of educational adequacy.

The Intelligence of Common Ground

"Public," as it is understood in this discussion, depends on two constructs of US democracy—universal and free—that undergird the intent of shared circumstance in public education. Universal and free are principles of "public" that "prepare all students to recognize and accept the basic equality among all persons, even as the achievement of this imperative is always a work in progress" (Reimers, 2006, p. 282). The role of public educators is to establish and maintain these conditions of shared circumstance.

Shared circumstance in public education begins with how educators model universal and free. Modeling occurs when all students experience a trusting relationship and learning experiences where they "acquire a sense of being valued and belonging that in a usually good environment builds to an increased capacity to learn; deepening human development" (Comer, 2015, p. 227).

Taking public education and US students beyond the confines of singularity, uncritical habits of mind, and the primacy of self-interest requires policy, power, and practice based on an understanding of successful intelligence. Successful intelligence (Sternberg and Grigorenko, 2004), as discussed earlier, is the array of capacities throughout analytical, creative, and practical intelligences that human beings apply to adapt, shape, and select environments. One of these capacities is *the intelligence of common ground*.

The intelligence of common ground is the province of public educators when the exchange between teaching and learning immerses students in principled reasoning. Educators take responsibility for investing in this capacity for "public" via caring classroom environments (Noddings, 2002) that "foster the child's construction of a worldview based on 'goodwill' (Arsenio and Lover, 1995) characterized by the presumption that social life operates for the most part according to basic moral principles of fairness and mutual respect" (Nucci, 2008, pp. 298–99).

Conditions established and responsibilities met by educators to create the intelligence of common ground establish public education as the crucible in which "public" is forged. Students express this capacity as *freedom vis-à-vis learning*.

Freedom vis-à-vis Learning

Freedom vis-à-vis learning is an expression of principled reasoning. The cognitive and moral wherewithal applied by individuals to recognize that "public" is the state of affairs where the benefits, goods, and rights of all maximize the rights of individuals lie at the core of freedom vis-à-vis learning. Self-mastery is fueled by this expression of principled learning because every person maximizes individual goods when all individuals exercise this freedom.

A simple example of freedom vis-à-vis learning appears when personal goods (wealth) are given up (taxes) as a matter of volition to gain the benefit of a community fire department. Freedom and the public good are acquired in this case because individuals are freed from the prohibitive expense of a personal fire department while all individuals benefit from shared cost for universal fire protection. This practical example, however, does not capture the depth of "public" established by freedom vis-à-vis learning.

A Sample Lesson: The Social Contract

Dynamic instruction in the intersection of moral obligation and the primary purpose of public education is a "teacher mediated process that assists students in effectively gaining the knowledge, skills, capabilities and moral dispositions that are of value in expanding their freedoms" (Reimers, 2006, p. 281). Freedom vis-à-vis learning is a capacity for intelligence of common ground exemplified by what is commonly referred to as the *social contract*.

Roughly speaking, the unwritten social contract is the agreement to choose the mutual benefit that accrues when every person ends the swinging of her/his arm while walking down the sidewalk at the point where another person's nose begins.

Intelligence of common ground is not derived from natural thinking. Uneducated meaning-making often chooses unlimited arm-swinging as if it constitutes freedom. The limitation of individual rights (unlimited arm-swinging) vouchsafes "public" and personal benefit of a greater good (uninjured noses of both passersby and the arm-swinger). Freedom—unimpeded and uninjured progress down the sidewalk—is the greater good of all encapsulated in an endless progression of undamaged noses afforded by the intelligence of common ground.

Attaining freedom vis-à-vis learning depends on accepting the argument that choosing a balance of individual and public goods cannot occur unless a community of teaching and learning is dedicated to the pursuit of multiple intelligences, cognitive agency, and "public" for all students (Swensson, Ellis, and Shaffer, 2019b). Embedded in this argument is the understanding that connections taught between principled reasoning, positive liberty, and moral obligation empower the capacities of choice-making for "public" exemplified by the social contract.

Engaging all students with care exemplars devoted to fulfillment of the moral obligation of public education via *how to think* means that freedom vis-à-vis learning within the intelligence of common ground facilitates the achievement of the public good. The common project of US public education for all students during the remainder of the twenty-first century is captured in this overarching dedication to the common ground of the greater good.

COMMON GROUND: "PUBLIC"

"Public" is acknowledgment of the need for intelligence of common ground. The need for and purpose of this iteration of human intelligence lie in a realization about the consequences of the disappearance of "public." As some researchers warn, American society faces challenges in a future where "all groups of children will be minorities living in a society polarized by race and poverty" (Orfield and Frankenberg, 2014, p. 724).

If "public" does not develop through learning the capacity to choose the cost to dispense with some individual goods in order to facilitate the public good, students face a future embedded in the past. "Public" as common ground eventuates when educational function incorporates sets that allow choices for dynamic instruction that engage students with learning experiences for balance, connection, and agency.

Balance and Common Ground

Balance is crafted when the original power of education *leads-out* care for others' interests and the potential, arising from this care, for working out differences. Sharing principles and working out differences yields balance in classrooms and public schools. Balance fosters legitimacy for an enduring community. Legitimacy is associated with fair participation, liberty and pluralism, equal opportunity, political/citizenship education, and professionalism/expertise (Knight Abowitz, 2011, p. 471).

Connection and Common Ground

The viability of "public" in US education for the remainder of the twenty-first century depends upon connection with lived experience across the diversity of America's students. Too often, the tendency in contemporary US education is to discard, ignore, or devalue diversity. Standardized testing, for example, functions "to force schools to adopt a standardized, non-multicultural curriculum, that ultimately silences the 'voices, the cultures, and the experiences of children' (McNeil, 2000, p. 232)" (Au, 2010, p. 6).

Instead of creating disconnection and thus making public school *subtractive* (Valenzuela, 2005), "public" is the active connection with the personal and cultural resources of students, families, and communities. Active connection allows classrooms and schools to create community for all students.

Put in a more practical way, *how to think* includes the cognitive behaviors of intelligences necessary to the moral obligation of public education to "help citizens talk to one another about shared problems in an attempt to find common ground and solutions" (Knight Abowitz, 2011, p. 478).

Agency and Common Ground

Common ground and common solutions develop if the rich cultural differences that strengthen meaning-making and provide resources for *how to think* are included as critique, intelligence, and solution during teaching and learning. Knowing "public" in this way allows the original power of education to be devoted to "a search for norms of justice people from different communities can share" (Strike, 2008, p. 119).

TWELVE
Weaving Educational Adequacy and the Good Public School

This search confirms that contemporary thinking about educational adequacy is the artistic equivalent of a toddler's stick-figure drawing. Contemporary understanding about educational adequacy and public education is one-dimensional and monochromatic. Politics, policy, and acrimony have rendered pictures of educational adequacy incomplete.

On behalf of all US students, educational adequacy and the good public school merit a more vibrant, more expressive, and more encompassing depiction.

The purpose of this chapter is to shed light on the determinants of twenty-first-century comprehensive public education. These constructs illuminate the multidimensional, polychromatic, interactive, and evolving nature of educational adequacy conspicuously absent from contemporary US education. These constructs are factors that decisively affect the nature of *21CPE*.

TRANSFORMING EDUCATIONAL ADEQUACY

If public educators are to utilize the constructs that decisively affect the nature of comprehensive public education, a heuristic is needed. The heuristic best suited to the professional expertise of public educators is Gunzenhauser's (2003) *philosophy of education*, which he defined as "a set of ideas and commitments about the purpose and value of education that guides our practice and helps us make choices" (p. 52).

COMMITMENTS ABOUT COMPREHENSIVE PUBLIC EDUCATION

Commitments about the purpose and value of education that emerge from this search suggest several general principles for a philosophy of comprehensive public education.

Principle #1: The first general principle is a day-to-day commitment to teaching and learning about intelligences and behaviors in "the realm of practical moral wisdom, a kind of professional virtue-in-action that could resemble 'moral case law'" (Campbell, 2008, p. 605). This principle is a commitment to the valorization of lived experience for all students, the flourishing of individuals invoked in a community that *leads-out* the assets each student brings to public school, and the freedom established for students when collective identity is vouchsafed and stereotype threat is eliminated.

Principle #2: Next, a primary purpose, *how to think*, is a commitment without which 21CPE cannot be realized. Not only is this primary purpose the fuel necessary to apply the values of the moral obligation of public education, but *how to think* yields the independent thinking necessary and sufficient for all intelligences to manifest principled reasoning and positive liberty. This principle is the progenitor of successful intelligence for all students.

Principle #3: The first two general principles are linked to a third. Professionally licensed public educators trained to build the intersection of primary purpose and moral obligation are a commitment because the beliefs of teachers have a profound impact on students. The beliefs of educators are related to student achievement. Educators influence students by "having a can-do attitude, knowing students' strengths and weakness, believing in making positive changes in students' lives, in addition to a host of motivational constructs such as commitment, persistence, and effort" (Lee and Shute, 2010, p. 195).

Principle #4: Dynamic instruction and its characteristics are commitments because "the relationship between pedagogical knowledge and student achievement appears to be empirically more strongly sustained" than the relationship between student achievement and the content knowledge of teachers (Mincu, 2015, p. 258). Studies also find that behavioral and cognitive engagement are fostered via teacher feedback, which "is among the most powerful influences on student learning and achievement" (Harbour et al., 2015, p. 9).

CHOICES, WEAVING, AND PHILOSOPHY

Commitments are a baseline from which public educators can evolve their philosophy of education to facilitate choices to transform the purpose of US public education. The complex interweaving of theory, pedagogy, and research brings to the fore a set of ideas relevant to a philosophy of education revealed during this search.

These threads (e.g., dynamic instruction, educational function, primary purpose, moral obligation, trust) constitute one set of ideas interwoven with commitments that transform purpose and depict value in a tapestry laden with RTS.

Evolving a philosophy of education to make choices and guide practice means that an educator's commitments and sets of ideas are central to transforming not only the purpose of public education but also the way that educational adequacy is understood and pursued. Among the ideas uncovered during this search for the good public school, several evoke the transformation of purpose and adequacy necessary and sufficient to engage all US students with the original power of education:

The responsibilities of educators—In the good public school, educators have, and will always have, essential responsibilities:

- To fulfill the moral obligation of public education and to pursue *how to think* through engaging all students with respect for all others.
- To valorize lived experience, collective identity, and "I identify as . . ." statements as the resources each student brings to class for engagement.
- To apply educational function to eliminate racial opportunity cost and stereotype threat.
- To engage professional capabilities, pedagogy, and emerging research to evolve a philosophy of education necessary to transform purpose and adequacy and sufficient to guide choices and practices that engage all students in comprehensive public education.

The value of moral obligation—Public educators begin to fulfill moral obligation with steadfast efforts to keep students physically safe. This is necessary but not sufficient to create the conditions necessary for comprehensive public education. Physical safety means little in terms of school success if fear attends any student's expression of self. The moral obligation of public education is to create safety for all students' "I identify as . . ." statements.

The moral obligation of public education and the extensive array of values that attend it are fulfilled when all classrooms are places where all students and their "I identify as . . ." statements "have the experience of care" (Strike, 2008, p. 129). Satisfactory quality emerges when communities in comprehensive public education foster freedom vis-à-vis learning to vouchsafe positive liberty. Choosing this level of moral obligation as the bedrock of educational adequacy creates "a community in which students are cared for and about generally and with respect to multiple domains of their lives" (Strike, 2008, p. 129).

The values of the moral obligation of public education rely upon *how to think* as the means to identify and pursue praiseworthy conceptions of the good. Studies indicate the power of choices that build the intersection between *how to think* and moral obligation. "Students have better academic outcomes when they have relationships with teachers that are more close and less conflictual (Birch and Ladd, 1997; Hamre and Piant, 2001; Ladd, Birch, and Buhs, 1999; Murray, 2009; Planta, Steinberg, and Rollins, 1995)" (Curby, Rimm-Kaufman, and Abry, 2013, p. 559).

Moral learning is normation—Because normation is that learning that creates a sense of justice as human behavior (Strike, 2008), choices about educational function, care, freedom, and student engagement are inextricably linked with a philosophy of education that supports *21CPE*.

Strike (2008) argues that "effective normation requires authoritative endorsement of the kind that is most effectively provided by strong communities characterized by a praiseworthy account of human flourishing and regulated by justifiable norms including norms of justice" (pp. 130–31). The educational choices that evoke human flourishing incorporate dynamic instruction as authoritative endorsement in a learning environment where care is omnipresent.

THE GOOD PUBLIC SCHOOL: INDICATORS AND OBJECTIVES

An authoritative tapestry that depicts comprehensive public education is woven using various threads of commitment, principle, and philosophy. The good public school combines these materials with indicators of, and objectives for, comprehensive public education.

21CPE *Indicators*

21CPE Indicators give educators opportunities to coordinate and choose facets of philosophy to craft educational adequacy and the good public school on behalf of their students. Indicators also give educators a baseline from which to assess the worth and the impact of their pursuit of comprehensive public education.

Commitment to purpose: Any purpose envisioned for public education has a dramatic impact on teaching and learning. Thus, the contemporary purpose of public education stymies the original power of education. Challenging this purpose and the conventional wisdom it represents is a commitment public educators must make; *how to think* must replace the status quo. No more important indicator of comprehensive public education exists.

Construction in the intersection: Dedication to educational adequacy is a promise and, as such, fulfillment of this promise depends upon persistent construction of the intersection between *how to think* and the moral obligation of public education. In this intersection is the reciprocal relationship of the exchange in the original power of education: *how to think* is agency for engaging with the values of moral obligation, and engagement in moral obligation validates the application of *how to think* so that this intersection becomes the origination point of freedom, independent thinking, principled reasoning, and positive liberty.

True North for Comprehensive Public Education: Contemporary US public education is a battleground, lightning rod, and societal conundrum. Command of the power of the "Why" of education is coveted. But command of education is misdirected; power is exercised as if it alone substantiates "right" and "either," and inadequacy flourishes.

Minkos et al. (2017) remind educators about the bidirectional influence of teaching and learning throughout the layers of experience and the circles of community that are integral to a student's life and capacities. Aligning community with the professional True North represented by commitments and sets of ideas in a philosophy of comprehensive public education is a priority if educational adequacy is to be transformed.

The local-ness of accountability: Internal accountability (Gunzenhauser, 2003) is an indicator to be exercised locally. The likelihood that internal accountability is feasible and part of the agency sufficient to the primary purpose of *21CPE* is confirmed by research findings that indicate that local accountability already exists. Marsh and Wohlstetter (2013) found that local actors in education take control of accountability through selective activation of elements of policy and by "directly challenging governance arrangements and defying traditional decision-making authority" (p. 278).

To lead-out: Simply put, the original power of education is to *lead-out*. The capacities of all students for intelligences that express the values of moral obligation grow during the exchange in the original power of education.

As this search discovered, however, education devoted to a purpose anchored in adult-centric singularity constrains, discriminates, and restricts. The tyranny of either/or—augmented by ideologies devoted to free market theory—exerts power over policy and politics to tighten the constraints of the contemporary purpose of education.

Constrained instruction focuses on test prep and knee-jerk pedagogy. Constrained, schools are disconnected from the greater good. A focus on the greater good emerges as an indicator that comprehensive public education is poised to engage all students with teaching and learning that evinces the social contract and freedom for all.

Indicators guide educators as they coordinate and choose among the professional resources, pedagogies, research, and characteristics of comprehensive public education. Connecting and applying these attributes of the philosophy for comprehensive public education occurs when several objectives are pursued. Objectives facilitate balance within comprehensive public education.

21CPE *Objectives*

Several objectives symbolize connections and applications that operationalize comprehensive public education. The good public school and educational adequacy are accessible throughout the remainder of this century when educators put philosophy and practice together to reach key objectives.

Objective #1: The Good School Is Functionally Public

As Stitzlein (2015) indicates, good schools must be *functionally public*. "Functionally public schools strive to develop a sense of 'we' collectively, but also an understanding of the well-being of individuals and their ability to pursue their own happiness" (p. 569).

As it's understood in this discussion, "public" is fostered when public educators engage all students with learning experiences that facilitate conjunction between positive liberty and the social contract. The purpose of the functionally public school is to establish "public" within the exchange between teaching and learning "where children learn how to express their ideas and respond to the ideas of others as they balance their own individual needs with collective needs" (Stitzlein, 2015, p. 567).

Pursuit of this objective connects several characteristics of the good public school:

- Within the original power of education, and the attributes it fosters in a functionally public school (e.g., the interweaving of dynamic instruction, effective evaluation, a strengths perspective, mutual valorization), lie the reduction of racial opportunity cost by "altering the school environment itself by narrowing the gap between the norms of the school and those of students' racial communities" (Chambers et al., 2014, p. 490).
- Educators dedicated to mediating identity establish a school environment of care, trust, moral obligation, and positive liberty.
- When all students learn *how to think* during authentic, identity-inclusive learning experiences, the intelligences of all students flourish.

Although every educator knows that a chain of command exercises authority and control beyond the school district (Au, 2010), the good public school must be functionally public to the extent that it exercises bidirectionality throughout local policy to take control of teaching and learning on behalf of all learners. To be functionally public, a good public school embraces what amounts to institutional self-mastery via locally sourced policy. This manifestation of efficacy permits education professionals and their schools to blend the ideal and the practical to drive the good public school forward.

Objective #2: The Good Public School Is How to Think

Either directly or indirectly, everything that happens in *21CPE* pursues a primary purpose: *how to think*. Because the intersection between primary purpose and the moral obligation of public education is the core of a functionally public school, the original power of education is exercised and maintained through this objective.

The overriding value of the primary purpose of the good public school is recognized in the scholarly agreement between sociologists and psychologists "that moral behavior entails cognitive understanding and the exercise of free will, not just imitating role models or ideals of virtue" (Snarey and Samuelson, 2008, p. 57).

Pursuit of this intersection during dynamic instruction (guided by educational function and the agency of the input-throughput-output cycle) sustains engagement of all students with habits of mind that fuel independent thinking and principled reasoning. Engagement with thinking skills is among the conditions that research indicates "strengthen Black students' will to achieve academically" (Hampton, 2016, p. 429).

Hampton (2016) indicates further that habits of mind like these promote community and interdependence that develop individual confidence to overcome systemic barriers.

Objective #3: The Good Public School Fulfills Moral Obligation

The fulfillment of the moral obligation of public education rests in the hands of public educators whose own "I identify as . . ." statements grow and mediate to incorporate the knowledge, cognitive process, integrity, and social justice sufficient to valorize the lived experience of all students.

Educators who successfully engage and build trust with students of color "assist students in negotiating and navigating through the system [and] provide support [to] help students build resiliency to work in the system and maintain their cultural identity and dignity (Garza, 1998; Scheurich, 1998; Valdez, 1996; Valenzuela, 1999)" (Garza and Garza, 2010, p. 204.

Socialization experiences built in this way in comprehensive public education are an intentional mix of decisions, choices, and behaviors that are relational, caring, integrity filled, and supportive of student, colleague, and family identities. These experiences are the kind of caring and mutually responsive relationships that give rise to conditions necessary for *secure attachment* (Lapsley, 2008). Secure attachment is the trusting relationship within the exchange at the core of the original power of education.

Secure attachment requires a persistent investment by educators in the choices and behaviors that evince care at a high level. This investment creates the conditions for student compliance with authoritative adult influence that engages them in authentic learning experiences in comprehensive public education. Compliance, in this sense, is an expression of self-regulation that evinces the mutuality within the original power of education. This exchange of intelligences is activated during dynamic instruction, and this mutuality is fostered by the care and concern of all educators for all students.

Objective #4: The Good Public School Is Student-Centric

Within a trust- and integrity-filled environment, students flourish as "teachers express warm feelings for children, offer nurturance for children's emotional and academic needs, and allow for developmentally appropriate levels of autonomy and responsibility in the classroom (Pianta, La Paro, and Hamre, 2008; Wentzel, 2002)" (Curby, Rimm-Kaufman, and Abry, 2013, p. 558). The capacities, lived experience, and prior learning of all students are the foundation of this objective.

The value of this objective is illustrated when teaching and learning in a comprehensive public school reflect the community-centered premise that "for human beings, most attitudes, behaviors, and skills are learned as a result of interactions with others within one's environment" (Hampton, 2016, p. 439).

As an example of this premise, an educator's responses to the "I identify as . . ." statements of students of color must support these as a plural subject for intergroup cohesion that constitutes "a social entity in which the members believe themselves to be obliged to believe and act together with those in their group" (Fraser-Burgess, 2012, p. 484).

Being student-centric, to extend this example, also means educators know that several studies indicate that "Black achievers manifest high levels of aspiration and have a perception of themselves involving the belief that they will accomplish the goals they set for themselves" (Hampton, 2016, p. 432). This objective puts public educators in the enviable position of engaging with a nuanced approach (the original power of education) to the nuances of the "I identify as . . ." statements of any and all students.

This discussion of the philosophy of comprehensive public education and tapestry of the good public school reveals that students also deserve learning experiences and environments that reflect up-to-date "neuroscience knowledge [because it] provides convincing evidence that it is brain-mind-environment interaction and development that determines learning capacities" (Comer, 2015, p. 230).

Objective #5: Directing the Power of Comprehensive Public Education

This search confirms that the original power of education is an amalgam, a weaving of choices and decisions during dynamic instruction to foster the exchange between intelligences in the intersection of primary purpose and moral obligation. Directing this power to maximize its effects on all students and their futures requires that educators array a number of core attributes of *21CPE* as objectives that activate, sustain, and direct the power of comprehensive public education:

- The moral obligation of public education cannot be separated from the moral conduct of adults in public education.
- A philosophy of education for the good public school must incorporate care, adequacy, and function unfettered by the classic systems model (I-P-O). Instead, a philosophy that orients practices chosen for the good public school must jettison the classic systems model and activate the model referred to by "the term IMOI (input-mediator-output-input)" (Ilgen et al., 2005, p. 520). Throughput is accounted for as "mediator" within this model, and a feedback loop develops as output segues to input and IMOI renews itself.
- The self-mastery of the good public school depends on what scholars refer to as the competent teacher's professional consciousness, "a kind of moral wisdom or judgement which is rooted in rational reflection about educational policies and practices and what is *ethically* (author's emphasis), as well as instrumentally, appropriate to achieve them (p. 265)" (Campbell, 2008, p. 604).
- The community that is a good school and that is a caring classroom invokes trust that "carries with it the affective connections of care, regulated by moral reciprocity, and continuity" (Nucci, 2008, p. 299).
- Power in *21CPE* is the professional agency of US educators that fulfills the moral obligation of public schools, valorizes the lived experience of all students, and engages all student capacities with *how to think*.
- The communities of any school must create trust to end deficit thinking, the impact of double consciousness, and the presence of stereotype threat. The tapestry for the good public school must share robust agency as the dedication of all staff to valorize the lived experience of all students and the capacities for meaning-making that students bring to the pursuit of *how to think*. Racial opportunity cost can never be levied again.
- This tapestry captures the locus of moral responsibility in public education as the persistent ethical conduct of educators (Campbell, 2008). Mediational influences and mediated identity weave the necessary and productive feedback and cycles that promote care, posi-

tive liberty, continuous improvement, and freedom vis-à-vis learning into the tapestry of comprehensive public education.

Educators direct the power of comprehensive public education to craft free and universal learning experiences for all students. Generating and applying a philosophy of comprehensive public education is the expression of the original power of education in an educator's professional tapestry woven from commitments, sets of ideas, indicators, and objectives. The capacity to evolve such a philosophy is the responsibility and True North of public educators during the remainder of the twenty-first century. The implications of this development spring from the implications associated with this search for educational adequacy.

THIRTEEN
Implications from This Search for Educational Adequacy

The primary implication of this search for educational adequacy is ironic. It turns out that satisfactory quality in the good public school requires a search that will never end.

The search that launched this discussion yields an inescapable conclusion: the foundational elements of *21CPE*—primary purpose, dynamic instruction, educational function, and moral obligation—are journeys, not destinations. As these journeys unfold, research, the IMOI (input-mediator-output-input) cycle (Ilgen et al., 2005), and the dialectic of the original power of education create the conditions for continuous improvement in teaching and learning.

As public educators acquire university-level professional training, gain experience, encounter and analyze data/research, and craft dynamic instruction, the search for educational adequacy in comprehensive public education makes progress but never ends. The interactive, reciprocating, dialectic within the exchange of intelligences woven within comprehensive public education is the momentum that transforms educational adequacy.

Both the good public school and twenty-first century educational adequacy constitute what scholars reference as *partially comprehensive doctrines*. A partially comprehensive doctrine shares characteristics "of what is valuable in human life, but it does not claim completeness and may coexist with other doctrines" (Strike, 2008, p. 125). This revelation, this primary implication of this search, entails further implications. These additional implications for teaching and learning are valuable in comprehensive public education and human life and are, simultaneously, persistently imperfect.

THE SECOND IMPLICATION

US public education must jettison adherence to the we-have-finally-made-it presumption that is responsible for acrimony, stasis, misdirection, and disconnection in contemporary public schooling. Those who manipulate policy and those who turn perspectives into ideology to acquire control over the original power of education restrict the search and pursuit that constitute the strength inherent in a partially comprehensive doctrine. Dissipating the fog of certainty becomes a priority for public educators once this implication is considered.

THE THIRD IMPLICATION

The challenges that face US students—"mobility, extreme poverty, a lack of shared resources" (Barnum, 2018a)—are omnipresent in public schools and classrooms. As a result, US public schools are called upon to meet a roster of basic human needs for students including physical and mental health needs, food insecurity needs, and clothing needs. Public education is expected to respond to family crises, gun violence, social media depredations, drug abuse, and a variety of other societal concerns.

Educators are called upon to meet needs and address issues that policy and politics have pushed into the school and classroom. Barriers, obfuscation, policy, cost-cutting, ideology, neglect, and politics have led to public education becoming a catch-all for the resolution of serious problems that schools are ill equipped to handle. Underfunded, understaffed, overwhelmed, yet, undaunted, educators deal with these tasks and the mandates that stretch, strain, and drain the original power of education.

The heroic efforts of public educators to meet student needs and respond to serious societal issues demonstrate enduring student-centric professionalism. These praiseworthy efforts, however, also signal that leaders and policymakers have left educators and their students with little time and less funding for teaching and learning suffused with satisfactory quality.

This implication is anything but subtle: the primary purpose and moral obligation of public education play second fiddle to the provision of services abandoned by public and governmental entities. US public educators now must engage with teaching and learning almost as an afterthought.

Although there is no question that these services must be provided and that these services are essential for the well-being of US students, there is significant concern that imposing the provision of these services on schools truncates the potential and reneges on the promises that lie at the center of public education.

THE FOURTH IMPLICATION

The next implication of this search is that steps must be taken to reinvigorate medical, mental health, social service, and other organizations to create networks dedicated to the broader good. To deliver on potential and promise, comprehensive public education can coordinate with, but cannot be the primary provider of, the support service network necessary to meet the health and welfare needs of students and their families.

To deliver the original power of education to all US students for the remainder of the twenty-first century means that social services for children and families must be coordinated with, but not offered by, comprehensive public education.

Revitalized social service networks are needed to benefit students and to allow comprehensive public education to have its maximum impact for all students and their futures. The restoration of society's obligation to provide services in support of families and children demands a transformation no less essential and no less thorough than the transformation of adequacy and purpose for US public education.

To this end, the revitalization of networks of social services begins with placement of these entities within:

- all local offices, campaign offices, and headquarters of each US representative;
- satellite offices of each US senator, and each governor;
- each US post office.

All of these locations will be equipped with a mini-clinic, open year-round, and from year to year, to meet the physical and mental health needs of students, families, and citizens. Partnerships with local hospitals and other health care providers will ensure that these locations have professional staff present from 9 a.m. through 9 p.m. seven days a week.

To fund service providers and to ensure the year-round availability of these networks, a public-good surcharge should be levied on a variety of existing organizations. Several organizations, whose mission statements espouse a desire to benefit all American citizens, ought to be contributors to this surcharge:

- National political parties—15 percent of the total dollars contributed to each national political party annually will fund the ongoing services provided by mini-clinics.
- PACs (Political Action Committee) regardless of their political genetics—15 percent of the total dollars raised annually will be used to fund both mini-clinics and the service and civic organizations that provide pre- and after-school services to students.
- Corporate members of ALEC (American Legislative Exchange Council), and similar ideologically based organizations—15 percent

of contributions annually will fund a School-Zone-MRE (Meals Ready to Eat) program (operated through existing religious, civic, or governmental entities on an after-school-hours basis) to provide evening and weekend meals to students.

To further fund the reinvigoration of community service networks and the agencies within them, state-level political parties will allocate $2 for every $10 contributed annually to community agencies in each network.

Private schools—institutions that are not part of the public schools sector but that for the most part are operated by religious bodies and, thus, benefit from tax-exempt status and/or state-supplied funding from free market mechanisms—can be tasked with working with these networked community agencies and institutions.

Private schools will further their faith-based missions by collaborating with agencies, foundations, and institutions whose work serves cohorts of students and families untouched by most private schools. Private schools can provide facilities and space on a collaborative basis to assist organizations to meet the needs of students and families during after-school and weekend hours. A priority will be given to training and hiring parents and caregivers of participating children (at a starting wage of $18/hour) to conduct the before- and after-school and School-Zone-MRE programs.

Instead of draining coffers using vouchers, tax credits, and other subsidies, private schools will revert to their important work teaching students whose families can afford to pay tuition from their own resources for exclusive schooling created by faith-based institutions. State funds for comprehensive public education will revert to serve students in traditional public schools.

Funding from vouchers, tax credits, and other governmental subsidies that currently are monopolized by families who can afford private education without government support will revert to salaries of educators in the public schools sector. Funding redirected to comprehensive public schools obviates the need for private schools to concern themselves about possible interference from government, including the expectations that attend state and federal subsidies.

THE FIFTH IMPLICATION

The implication from this search is that educators must commit to the pursuit of the foundational elements of comprehensive public education at the local level on behalf of all students.

Making this commitment entails the embrace of "a both-and logic that acknowledges the reality of irony and paradox and the contingency and fluidity of boundaries . . . [and] the messy, intractable realities of schools and classrooms" (Granger, 2008, p. 224). Instead of a formula, template, or recipe, locally crafted common ground develops continuously during and because of the pursuit of foundational elements necessary and sufficient to the learning and futures of all US students in *21CPE*.

THE SIXTH IMPLICATION

The final implication of this search is that the futures of all US students depend on public educators adopting common ground for educational adequacy in public education. Common ground for comprehensive public education is vested in

- the intersection of *how to think* and the moral obligation of public education.
- dynamic instruction and educational function.
- transformed educational adequacy and the original power of education.
- a revitalized and fully funded coalition of social service providers to meet the needs of US students.

LEARNING FROM THE IMPLICATIONS OF THIS SEARCH

The implications of this search are teachable moments. Educators and supporters of the transformation of educational adequacy have the obligation to understand and share the learning that emerges from this discussion.

- The tyranny of either/or is anathema to the primary purpose of comprehensive public education. The implication from this search is that policy, practice, and politics in America's public schools must seek common ground instead of struggling to emblazon one perspective or another as "right." Contemporary US education is out of balance because this struggle continues.
- The power of US public education is diffused and fragmented unless a primary purpose for teaching and learning is identified. The primary purpose of *21CPE* stipulated within this discussion constitutes both an identification of and an allegiance to student-centric teaching and learning. *How to think* as a primary purpose puts The Public on notice about both educational adequacy and educational function as factors that measure a good school.
- When scholars indicate that "moral identity is open to revision across the life course" (Lapsley, 2008, p. 40), they suggest the multiple virtues of establishing *how to think* as the primary purpose of *21CPE*. An individual's ability to bring successful intelligence and moral purpose to life's vicissitudes depends on habits of mind.

Good schools in the twenty-first century are the bedrock from which student engagement can grow to evince cognitive and moral behaviors that express and promote balance between individual and public goods.

- Community and culture play vibrant roles in public education. This search teaches, first, that public schools are communities amid communities. Next, this search teaches that the community or group that is a public school instills "group identification [that] is not simply awareness that one is a member of a group, but rather that one is responsible for the group" (Lapsley, 2008, p. 38). This depiction teaches that the conjunction of "I identify as . . ." statements with the greater good are community within a good school.
- "I identify as . . ." statements, natural thinking, and meaning-making are powers that each student possesses. This search teaches that students are validated through the community at the intersection of primary purpose and moral obligation that activates "the rational, intentional nature of distinctly moral functioning, and [the] integration of self and identity with moral rationality and responsibility" (Lapsley, 2008, p. 37).
- *How to think* crafted via the original power of education establishes the habits of mind identified by Hampton (2016), the capacity invoked by Roosevelt (1937), and the personal liberty stipulated by Fraser-Burgess (2012), as the ethical, emotional, behavioral, and cognitive agency necessary and sufficient for all students to withhold their consent to marginalization, discrimination, and hate.
- The primary purpose of comprehensive public education lends lived experience, the assets of individuals, meaning-making, and natural thinking the power necessary to ward off ideas and individuals and groups whose intent is to marginalize. *How to think* fosters and fuels independent thinking, principled reasoning, and personal liberty, as capabilities all students can apply to assert, sustain, and/or defend their "I identify as . . ." statements.
- Marginalization of any student for any reason signifies the rejection of the moral obligation of public education. This search provides a teachable moment about educational function and dynamic instruction that entail the pedagogy necessary to nurture what Hampton (2016) refers to as the successful learner characteristics evinced by students of color: self-respect, command of standard English, goal-setting ability, self-motivation, time management skills, consequence awareness, and respect for others (pp. 425–26). The good public school does not exist if any student is subject to deficiencies or disparities.
- Practicalities accompany the transformation of educational adequacy. These practicalities teach how the intents of universal and free

must be accessible to all students in all schools that receive public funding:

- enroll all students regardless of disabilities, race, country of origin, first language, socioeconomic status;
- eliminate fees or up-charges that make enrollment prohibitive for some families;
- maximize enrollment without regard to when a student seeks to enroll during the course of a school year; and
- abandon "no excuses" punishments for bodily needs or achievement difficulties (Shapiro, 2018, p. 6).

- Standardized achievement testing is a failure of measurement, and this failure erodes the legitimacy of US public education. Because the mantle of accountability has been bestowed upon standardized testing, the data from these assessments is taken at face value. When critics of public education and policymakers apply these results as if they are a legitimate measure of educational adequacy and the original power of education, schools and school districts lose legitimacy in the eyes of the public. Effective evaluation emerges as a priority from this teachable moment.
- This search reveals that public education in the United States must fulfill numerous responsibilities. Among these is the responsibility for educational function, dynamic instruction, and care that acknowledges "all members of the nation and their rights, thereby working against the tyranny of the majority and establishing a precedent of concern for the well-being of minorities" (Stitzlein, 2015, p. 570).
- The exchange of intelligences at the center of the original power of education is facilitated when a coordinated, intentional, multifaceted support system exists for all students without draining the original power of education in *21CPE*. This teachable moment reveals that funding must be addressed for reconfigured social service networks that foster educational adequacy in *21CPE*. One of the most obvious implications arising from this search is that society's obligation to the futures of US children is underfunded. This state of affairs cannot continue if all students are to experience the satisfactory quality in learning and teaching that they deserve.

Teachable Moments and Legitimacy for 21CPE

"All organizations must maintain institutional legitimacy in order to preserve their status and ensure the continued provision of resources (Di Maggio and Powell, 1983)" (Jacobson, Snyder, and Saultz, 2014, p. 2). The teachable moments that emerge from this discussion are among the resources that educators and public school proponents must self-own.

To restore legitimacy, effective evaluation in *21CPE* must assess *how to think* so that teachers can respond to students with dynamic instruction that remediates, enriches, and segues to new learning. Cognition and engagement that develop for all students in the intersection of primary purpose and moral obligation are the "what's taught" during comprehensive public education. Effective evaluation of "what's taught" allows the dialectic of dynamic instruction to inform educators about how best to sustain and grow the academic success of each student.

Public educators have a level of responsibility that derives from "a sense of obligation and a concern for the consequences of one's actions" (Stitzlein, 2015, p. 572). Learning from this search includes the realization that a good school and the educators who make it functionally public must exercise a level of responsibility worthy of care exemplars.

FOURTEEN
Student Futures and Comprehensive Public Education

> The source of America's prosperity has never been merely how ably we accumulate wealth, but how well we educate our people.
> —Ikpa, 2016, p. 470

Instead of concluding with an exclamation of *Eureka!*, this search for educational adequacy comes to the crest of a hill to find that just ahead is another hill overgrown with ideas and research to improve teaching and learning. Instead of ending by identifying scapegoats or rounding up the usual suspects, this search for educational adequacy also reveals the imperative for transformation. Instead of deferring to minimums substituting for adequacy and instead of acquiescing to an archaic purpose, this search for the good public school identifies the tipping point for transformation.

It is time to alter fundamentally the trajectory of educational adequacy in US public education. The futures that all students deserve cannot continue to ignore that minimums are a self-fulfilling prophecy for teaching and learning. The purpose of this chapter is to take the initiative to crest the next hill, transform perceptions of educational adequacy, and welcome the future for all US students to the good public school.

WE HAVE MET THE ENEMY AND HE IS US

Multiple examples of what not to do, multiple examples of disconnected policy, multiple examples of insufficient funding, multiple examples of deficit thinking, multiple examples of missed educational opportunities litter the history of US schools. Amid this clutter and emerging from this discussion is a suggestion about the peril and the potential of the double-edged sword of power in education. The extent to which educational inadequacy is self-inflicted, and the extent to which enduring transformation of this wound is possible, exist side by side.

The inadequacies of contemporary US education and the necessity for transforming educational adequacy are captured in the time-honored epigram originally featured on a 1970 poster for Earth Day: "We have met the enemy and he is us" (Bush, 2014). As this phrase suggests, educators, leaders, and policymakers are responsible for inadequacy within the current state of affairs. But the responsibility communicated by this phrase also represents capabilities of public educators to transform what now fails to live up to the potential in the original power of education.

Stasis versus Transformation

The stasis that typifies contemporary US education emerged throughout this search for the good public school. With educational adequacy mired in minimums, stasis is the unavoidable avatar of decisions, choices, legislation, funding, and practice that enables the inadequacies that are the enemy of bright futures for all US students.

But tenets of a philosophy of education arise throughout this discussion. Initially, these transform how educational adequacy is understood. Further, these foster the realization that the search for the good public school is never-ending. On behalf of all US students, educators must take responsibility for seeking, shaping, and implementing these tenets to engage all students with the power of freedom necessary for fulfilling futures.

The First Tenet: Power

The first tenet of a philosophy of comprehensive public education is that education is power. This power is not rooted in politics, ideology, or funding, however. Instead, power is the exchange created between intelligences in classrooms where dynamic instruction engages all students with the intersection of *how to think* and the moral obligation of public education.

The power of teaching and the power of learning are reciprocal. Each student's power of cognitive ownership is enhanced and challenged when engaged by the power of teaching.

This exercise of power is solely within the professional purview of public educators. This original power of education is the efficacy required to craft 21CPE and to benefit every student. This power exemplifies the argument that connections taught between principled reasoning, positive liberty, and moral obligation empower the capacities of choice making for "public," the social contract, and the transformed definition of educational adequacy.

The Second Tenet: True North

True North for *21CPE* is the investment of educators in community. The original power of education is necessary and sufficient to make this investment because this exchange between intelligences establishes freedom vis-à-vis learning. Freedom vis-à-vis learning is self-regulation within community so that an individual does "not attach any sense of superior value to his cultural, ethnic, or racial identity but would instead see himself as a compound of several contingencies that make up the identity he had (Hill, 2000, 121)" (Reimers, 2006, p. 283).

Self-regulation is strengthened from the convergence of continuous improvement and positive liberty. Continuous improvement is a capacity evinced when educators implement the IMOI (input-mediator-output-input) cycle (Ilgen et al., 2005) and the dialectic in the original power of education. Positive liberty, the "freedom to be ruled by the dictates of one's own reason" (Fraser-Burgess, 2012, p. 487), is each student's expression of independent thinking, principled reasoning, and the values of the moral obligation of public education.

When educators make decisions about teaching and learning in pursuit of this convergence, True North becomes the journey that typifies the search at the heart of *21CPE*.

The Third Tenet: Principled Reasoning

Principled reasoning is learned when dynamic instruction engages all students with habits of mind in the intersection of primary purpose and moral obligation. Principled reasoning, for the purposes of this discussion, is the interplay between cognition and behavior that expresses the values of the moral obligation of public education in relationship with "public" during a student's True North journey.

Principled reasoning, thus, is the origin of capacities for both educators and students that ensure praiseworthy conceptions of the good are anchored by the understanding that "other cultural views are recognized as such and deliberation involves acknowledging the respective reasons of the various cultural views, then selecting the rules that establish fair terms of cooperation based on reconciling the evidence and reasons" (Fraser-Burgess, 2012, pp. 497–98).

The Fourth Tenet: Critical Habits of Mind

Idios (the Greek root of "idiocy," which means "private, self-centered, selfish, and separate" [Au, 2010, p. 8]) has no place in comprehensive public education. Community, self-regulation, principled reasoning, and the original power of education expressed throughout *21CPE* eschew singularity in favor of critical habits of mind, including those that make possible "standards of fairness, the rights of individuals and [those] with regard to accepting and addressing differences among individuals and cultural groups" (Reimers, 2006, p. 280).

The Fifth Tenet: Common Ground

Common ground is the baseline from which educators exert their power for policy, practice, and professionalism embedded in comprehensive public education. Common ground embraces locally sourced policy as the student-centric and bidirectional means for the evolution of educational adequacy. The good public school emerges when the intelligence of common ground is fostered in the exchange between teaching and learning.

Restoring "public" is possible when the intelligence of common ground develops within caring classroom environments (Noddings, 2002). 21CPE environments are designed to "foster the child's construction of a worldview based on 'goodwill' (Arsenio and Lover, 1995) characterized by the presumption that social life operates for the most part according to basic moral principles of fairness and mutual respect" (Nucci, 2008, pp. 298–99). Common ground is the good school and educational adequacy attuned to the positive consequences of the restoration of "public" throughout American society.

THE BENCHMARKS FOR 21CPE

Benchmarks for comprehensive public education give educators the ability to make decisions allied with the transformed definition of educational adequacy and the persistent pursuit of the tenets of the educational philosophy of a good public school. The good public school is identified by the extent to which these benchmarks establish, sustain, and grow the attributes of the original power of education on behalf of all students:

Clarity and agency. Good public schools articulate "clear expectations, establish instructional coherence across classrooms, and provide consistent and constructive feedback to students (Jang et al., 2010)" (Adams et al., 2016, p. 172). Agency in comprehensive public education revealed during this discussion is the wellspring provided by educational function and dynamic instruction for learning, each student's power of cognitive ownership.

When clarity and agency are omnipresent, teaching and learning exhibit the exchange that takes students beyond uncritical habits of mind and the primacy of self-interest into the intelligence of social balance. This aspect of intelligence is agency of the intentional self for each student.

Acquired student capacities. The good public school immerses all students in educational experiences that transform each student's cognitive ownership. Responsive and dialectic, these experiences engage all students (behaviorally, cognitively, and emotionally) with authentic learning via dynamic instruction about critical habits of mind. Students thus engaged access and acquire the capacities (e.g., independent thinking, principled reasoning) for being ruled by their own wisdom, which is the exercise of freedom, self-mastery, and the intelligence of common ground.

Public education writ large is socialization, qualification, and subjectification (Biesta, 2009). Learning, each student's cognitive ownership, acquires the capacities necessary and sufficient to self-valorize, fend off marginalization, and evoke the social contract in response to these three educational inevitabilities.

Intelligence of social balance. This search for educational adequacy suggests that behaviors aligned with the social contract encompass intelligences that facilitate choices to pay the cost of limited individual arm-swinging to enjoy the universal freedom of unbroken noses. Agency necessary and sufficient to bring these intelligences to the fore represents the ultimate expression of democracy-attached: social justice.

Because social justice "implies that persons have an obligation to be active and productive participants in the life of society and that *society has a duty to enable them to participate in this way*" (emphasis original) (Reisch, 2002, p. 346), the common project of *21CPE* puts successful intelligence, the intelligence of social balance, the values of the moral obligation of public education, and freedom/universality at the disposal of future members of society—public school students—so that their participation in the life of society is the impetus to facilitate the duty of society.

Common project and transformed adequacy. Although contemporary public education and *21CPE* differ in many ways, they share one attribute: public education is the common project of American democracy.

Adapting, shaping, and selecting democratic environments is "a common project that is pursued out of a commitment to some larger good and where love and compassion for one another are a part of this common project" (Strike, 2008, p. 128). To achieve this level of satisfactory quality, *21CPE* transforms the common project of "public" fostered by moral obligation and the original power of education: *educational adequacy is successful intelligence for a democracy*.

School attached, democracy attached. As Stizlein (2015) indicates, the essence of "public" is a shared circumstance of people "connected by common concerns about their shared fate, care for the interests of others, and the desire to seek shared principles that enable them to work out differences" (p. 566). Pedagogical agency in comprehensive public education to teach this level of successful intelligence begins with the understanding that all students are school attached.

A dedication to ensuring that all students are school attached is the foundation for relatedness and trust so that secure attachment is each student's investment in the original power of education. School attached also means that principles of "public" "prepare all students to recognize and accept the basic equality among all persons, even as the achievement of this imperative is always a work in progress" (Reimers, 2006, p. 282). This investment and this recognition signal a good public school.

Universal and free are forever the intent of American public schools. Fulfilling this intent entails a conjunction between the social contract and social justice that is expressed by graduates of *21CPE* when they are ruled by the dictates of their own reason to choose to be society-and-democracy attached.

Power and educational adequacy. Reciprocity represents the power of teaching in the exchange of intelligences capable of fostering principled reasoning, positive liberty, school attached and democracy attached. Educators express this power as collective efficacy originating in a "shared interest in advancing the education and well-being of children in order to help them work through inevitable differences and conflicts" (Knight Abowitz, 2011, p. 487).

PROMISES EMPOWER *21CPE*

The promises made when educators actively pursue a transformed definition of educational adequacy to ensure a good public school for all students put educators and students in position to engage with "a capacity for a conception of the good, and a capacity for a sense of justice" (Strike, 2008, p. 119).

This capacity brings another promise to the forefront of *21CPE*: the restoration of political legitimacy to the exercise of comprehensive public education. Knight Abowitz (2011) enumerates five principles of political legitimacy of public education in our democracy: fair participation, liberty and pluralism, equal opportunity, political education, and professionalism (p. 471). These five are embedded within the values of the moral obligation of *21CPE* and the characteristics of the transformed definition of educational adequacy.

The promises of *21CPE* include constructing learning environments from "judgements about what is educationally *desirable*" (Biesta, 2009, p. 2). Instead of grounding education in political or ideological imperatives, implementation of the original power of education means what is educationally desirable is the common project of US public education. The bottom line about what is educationally desirable for all students is taking them beyond a rudimentary understanding of knowledge, habits of mind, and concepts to "use them appropriately, e.g., apply them to a new situation, analyze data and draw appropriate conclusions, or evaluate the validity of information" (Jensen et al., 2014, p. 312).

Alongside these promises is the promise to take public education away from ideology as destiny where "either" and "or" substitute for praiseworthy conceptions of the good. This promise connotes the necessity for public educators to end division, exclusion, and segregation. This promise also connotes the necessity for future educational policy to end dissension and the conflict between perspectives in favor of the intelligence of common ground. Policy focused on fair participation facilitates political legitimacy and engagement with what is educationally desirable.

Perhaps the most dramatic promise is the agency accepted and embraced by comprehensive public educators when they act as policymakers to transform, persistently, *21CPE*. After all, "Policy makers can present compelling arguments to legislators and other officials, based on the plentitude of research findings" (Cohen et al., 2009, p. 204). Locally sourced policy, collaborative networks of school boards and educational associations, a national focus piloted by an AEA, and the full scope of promises in *21CPE* constitute the potential for the futures that all US students deserve from the good public school.

Freedom in Comprehensive Public Education

Freedom is a promise made by American democracy. Freedom that is often missing from the nation's history and from the lives of too many US students becomes a promise to which comprehensive public education is beholden.

The interactive balance in the exercise of the social contract and the exchange of intelligences that constitutes the original power of education engage lived experience and positive liberty "with the larger social reality, providing a richly contextual way of contributing to a concrete but dynamic (i.e., experimental) social good in which all might share" (Granger, 2008, p. 223).

Freedom is a social good capable of speaking power to uncritical habits of mind. For instance, freedom vis-à-vis learning connotes the fulfillment of the moral obligation of public education when educators and students honor the "I identify as . . ." statements of all in the school community. Critical habits of mind segue with the research that indicates "that there are multiple identity profiles—some of which are individual and some of which are dual in focus—which predict different educational outcomes" (Worrell, 2014, p. 342).

Freedom emerges from the intersection between primary purpose and moral obligation as a community investment in the power of principled reasoning that incorporates "educational resiliency: building confidence, making connections, setting goals, managing stress, increasing well-being, and understanding motivation" (Hampton, 2016, p. 428).

Achieving the public good amid diversity is a challenge that endures in America. As one crucial element in developing and sustaining the capacity of individuals to bear the costs of forswearing some individual goods to choose the public good, comprehensive public education is tasked with embracing the transformation of educational adequacy to engage all students with learning experiences that honor the fact that "there is not a singular narrative of America, but multiple, complex social histories told from diverse perspectives" (Malin, 2011, p. 114).

The universality of diversity is America's present and future. Social justice, therefore, is the universality fostered by student engagement with independent thinking, principled reasoning, and positive liberty. These exemplars of freedom permit balance between individual and public goods as common ground for the freedom of all individuals. America's schools have a moral obligation to ensure that all students' capabilities incorporate *how to think*. Establishing this primary purpose for the future of US public education gives all students the autonomy of self-mastery and positive liberty alongside myriad opportunities afforded by the social contract.

DEALING WITH THE "IF" OF 21CPE

21CPE is not a foregone conclusion. If comprehensive public education is to develop, if 21CPE is to serve all US students, and if a transformed definition of educational adequacy is to guide the good public school throughout America, public educators and the proponents of public education are responsible for directing their capacities to marshal the ideas encountered throughout this discussion.

Effective arrangement of and engagement with the concepts, policies, and practices necessary and sufficient to establish 21CPE depend on public educators taking account of and responding to several practical considerations:

- Policymaking is responsible for myriad backward demands "placed on the school from external audiences (e.g., accountability standards mandated by state education agencies) that threaten coherence and successful school improvement (Honig and Hatch, 2004; Hoppey, 2006; Newmann et al., 2000)" (Waldron and McLeskey, 2010, p. 68).
- A fundamental strength of public school educators that Goodson (2007) articulates, "I would suggest that we underestimate the self-sacrificing sense of mission of so many public service workers at our peril" (p. 147), is the power available for policymaking on behalf of 21CPE.

- "We do know that race-conscious school choice policies, while not perfect, are much more successful at creating diverse and high-quality public schools and a more balanced and equal educational system (see Holme and Wells 2009)" (Roda and Wells, 2013, p. 287).
- Marsh and Wohlstetter (2013) indicate the viability of locally sourced policymaking to support *21CPE* because existing school districts "have at times established considerable independence from federal policymakers by evading or modifying policy to meet local needs (Berman and McLaughlin, 1977, p. 277)."

WELCOME TO THE GOOD PUBLIC SCHOOL

The good public school, like a philosophy of education, "is never complete; it is constantly enriched by reflection and ongoing conversation" (Gunzenhauser, 2003, p. 52).

Meaning-making and lived experience represent the initial capacities that all students bring to all classrooms. These resources symbolize the evolving nature of learning and the ever-present ability of students to exchange intelligences during dynamic instruction. The good public school constructs an intersection of primary purpose and moral obligation where the resources that all students bring to class are nurtured and grown. Critical habits of mind become the building blocks for principled reasoning, positive liberty, and independent thinking.

The good public school incorporates these elements in alignment with the transformation of educational adequacy and so that "the special human capacity for 'theory of mind' [which] allows us to appreciate that we may have different perspectives and concerns" (Mercer, 2013, p. 163) becomes a hallmark of *21CPE*.

The good public school and good educational policy embrace diversity because, as research illuminates, diversity is a keystone for multiple "benefits, not only in test scores but also in important outcomes such as high school graduation, success in college, and being prepared to live and work in inter-racial settings as adults (Linn and Welner, 2007; Mickelson and Nkomo, 2012)" (Orfield and Frankenberg, 2014, p. 724).

When policy is locally sourced—generated from the bottom-up—educators can espouse the value of "their own local understandings of the conditions that do and do not contribute to educational improvement and to interrogate those understandings" (Honig and Coburn, 2007, p. 602). The good public school is built when educators establish community in each classroom and throughout each school. In this way, the good public school serves as a place "where individuals pursue their own liberties while simultaneously upholding those of others" (Stitzlein, 2015, p. 567). This is the capacity for freedom in the good public school.

The intended relationship between US democracy and traditional public education is sustained (Dewey, 1916; Knight Abowitz, 2011; Stitzlein, 2015; Swensson, Ellis, and Shaffer, 2019a) and grown when 21CPE is pursued. The transformation of educational adequacy not only advances this relationship but also gives public education a clear goal-in-mind throughout every lesson.

Critical habits of mind symbolize the power of primary purpose of comprehensive public education to evoke shared circumstance, positive liberty, the balance of social intelligence, and the intelligence of common ground. Democracy cannot live up to its intentions and promises unless comprehensive public education is an educational environment where the greater good is the greatest good for each student.

The understanding that "children's development occurs as a function of their interactions with their environment (Bronfrenbrenner and Morris, 2006)" (Curby, Rimm-Kaufman, and Abry, 2013, p. 568) underlies the pursuit of this relationship in the good public school.

The transformation of educational adequacy is an investment in the original power of education that distinguishes comprehensive public education. From this investment, the moral obligation of public education pays a dividend of the intentional self.

Not only does this dividend encompass agency that constitutes an increase in an individual's "sense of being in charge, of being capable and responsible, a master of one's domain" (Lapsley, 2008, p. 36), but this dividend compounds via freedom vis-à-vis learning. The intentional self is a bulwark against marginalization. The intentional self is an expression of the combined power of critical habits of mind and the social contract. The good public school engages all students with experiences that foster this combination.

Educational adequacy transformed facilitates and nurtures the conditions of community where the good public school is functionally public. The purpose of the functionally public school is to establish "public" within the exchange between teaching and learning "where children learn how to express their ideas and respond to the ideas of others as they balance their own individual needs with collective needs" (Stitzlein, 2015, p. 567).

All US students deserve the futures they create from learning experiences provided during 21CPE. The transformation of educational adequacy gives rise to the good public school. The concepts uncovered during this search and the professional acumen of public educators provide the framework from which transformation can begin. On behalf of every US student, let the pursuit of twenty-first century comprehensive public education begin.

References

Acton, Lord [Dalberg-Acton, John Emerich Edward]. (n.d.). Lord Acton Quote Archive. *Acton Institute.* Retrieved from https://acton.org.

Adams, C. M., Ware, J. K., Miskell, R. C., and Forsyth, P. B. (2016). Self-Regulatory Climate: A Positive Attribute of Public Schools. *The Journal of Educational Research (109)*2, 169–80. Retrieved from http://dx.doi.org/10.1080/00220671.2014.934419.

Anyon, J. (2005). What "Counts" as Educational Policy? Notes toward a New Paradigm. *Harvard Educational Review (75)*1, 65–88. Retrieved from https://doi.org/10.17763/haer.75.1.g1q5k721220ku176.

Au, W. (2010). The Idiocy of Policy: The Anti-Democratic Curriculum of High-Stakes Testing. *Critical Education (1)*1, 1–15. Retrieved from https://doi.org/10.14288/ce.v1i1.182239.

Barnum, M. (2017). Beyond the Test Score Horse Race: 5 Big Questions Researchers Are Asking about Charter Schools. *Chalkbeat.* June 15, 2017. Retrieved from https://www.chalkbeat.org/posts/us/2017/06/15/beyond-the-test-score.

Barnum, M. (2018a). Why One Harvard Professor Calls American Schools' Focus on Testing a "Charade." *Chalkbeat.* January 19, 2018. Retrieved from https://www.chalkbeat.org/posts/us/2018/01/19/why-one-harvard-professor.

Barnum, M. (2018b). Virtual Schools, Open Records, and Claims about Research—Highlights from Congress's Look at Charter Schools. *Chalkbeat.* June 13, 2018. Retrieved from http://www.chalkbeat.com/posts/us/2018/06/13/virtual-schools-open.

Beyer, B. K. (2008a). How to Teach Thinking Skills in Social Studies and History. *The Social Studies 99*(5), 196–201. September/October 2008.

Beyer, B. K. (2008b). What Research Tells Us about Teaching Thinking Skills. *The Social Studies 99*(5), 223–32. September/October 2008.

Biesta, G. (2009). Good Education in an Age of Measurement: On the Need to Reconnect with the Question of Purpose in Education. *Educational Assessment, Evaluation and Accountability (21)*1, 33–46. Retrieved from https://doi.org/10.1007/s11092-008-9064-9.

Bloom, B. (Ed.) (1956). *Taxonomy of Educational Objectives: The Classification of Educational Goals.* New York: Longmans Green.

Bonner, E. P. (2014). Investigating Practices of Highly Successful Mathematics Teachers of Traditionally Underserved Students. *Educational Studies in Mathematics 86*(3), 377–99. doi:10.1007/s10649-014-9533-7.

Bourdieu, P. (1982). Les rites d'institution. *Actes de la recherché en sciences sociales 43*, 58–63.

Brown, F. (2002). Privatization of Public Elementary and Secondary Education in the United States of America. *Education and the Law (14)*1–2, 99–114. doi:10.1080/09539960220149218.

Brown, P. C., Roediger III, H. L., and McDaniel, M. A. (2014). *Make It Stick: The Science of Successful Learning.* Cambridge, MA: The Belknap Press of Harvard University Press.

Brown v. Board of Education, 347 U.S. 483 (1954).

Burch, P. (2007). Educational Policy and Practice from the Perspective of Institutional Theory: Crafting a Wider Lens. *Educational Researcher (36)*2, 84–95.

Bush, L. (2014). The Morphology of a Humorous Phrase: "We have met the enemy and he is us." Retrieved from https://humorinamerica.wordpress.com.

Buszin, J. S. (2012–2013). Beyond School Finance: Refocusing Education Reform Litigation to Realize the Deferred Dream of Education Equality and Adequacy. *Emory Law Journal 62*, 1613–57.

Campbell, E. (2008). Teaching Ethically as a Moral Condition of Professionalism. In Larry P. Nucci and Darcia Narvaez (Eds.), *Handbook of Moral and Character Education*, 601–15. New York: Routledge.

CAPE (Council for American Private Education). (2018). Facts and Studies. Retrieved from www.capenet.org.

Chambers, T. V., Huggins, K. S., Locke, L. A., and Fowler, R. M. (2014). Between a "ROC" and a School Place: The Role of *Racial Opportunity Cost* in the Educational Experiences of Academically Successful Students of Color. *Educational Studies 50*, 464–97. doi: 10.1080/00131946/2014.943891.

Charalambos, C. Y., and Hill, H. C. (2012). Teacher knowledge, curriculum materials, and quality of instruction: Unpacking a complex relationship. *Journal of Curriculum Studies (44)4*, 443–66. doi: 10.1080/00220272.2011.650215.

Chen, G. (2018). White Students Are Now the Minority in US Public Schools. *Public School Review*. September 4, 2018. Retrieved from www.publicschoolreview.com.

Chubb, J. E., and Moe, T. M. (1990). *Politics, Markets, and America's Schools*. Washington, DC: The Brookings Institution.

Cohen, J., McCabe, E. M., Michelli, N. M., and Pickeral, T. (2009). School Climate: Research, Policy, Practice, and Teacher Education. *Teachers College Record (111)1*, 180–213.

Comer, J. P. (2015). Developing Social Capital in Schools. *Society 52*, 225–31. doi: 10.1007/s12115-015-9891-5.

Curby, T. W., Rimm-Kaufman, S. E., and Abry, T. (2013). Do Emotional Support and Classroom Organization Earlier in the Year Set the Stage for Higher Quality Instruction? *Journal of School Psychology 51*(5), 557–69. Retrieved from http://dx.doi.org/10.1016/j.sp.2013.06.001.

David, R., and Hesla, K. (2018). Estimated Public Charter School Enrollment 2017–2018. National Alliance for Public Charter Schools. March 2018. Retrieved from www.publiccharters.org.

DeAngelis, C. A., and Erickson, H. H. (2018). What Leads to Successful School Choice Programs? A Review of the Theories and Evidence. *Cato Journal (38)1*, 247–60.

Dewey, J. (1916). *Democracy and Education*. Retrieved from www.public-library.uk.

De Witte, K., and Rogge, N. (2016). Problem-Based Learning in Secondary Education: Evaluation by an Experiment. *Education Economics (24)1*, 58–82. http://dx.doi.org/10.1080/09645292.2014.966061.

Diamond, J. B., and Huguley, J. P. (2014). Testing the Oppositional Culture Explanation in Desegregated Schools: The Impact of Racial Differences in Academic Orientations on School Performance. *Social Forces (93)2*, 747–77. doi: 10.1093/sf/sou093.

DuFour, R., and Marzano, R. (2011). *Leaders of Learning: How District, School, and Classroom Leaders Improve Student Achievement*. Bloomington, IN: Solution Tree Press.

Eastman, J. (2017). Regaining Trust in Nonprofit Charter Schools: Toward Benefit Corporation Branding for For-Profit Education Management Organizations. *BYU Education and Law Journal* (2), 285–324.

Ely, T. L., and Teske, P. (2015). Implications of Public School Choice for Residential Location Decisions. *Urban Affairs Review (51)2*, 175–204. doi: 10.1177/1078087414529120.

Eng, N. (2013). The Impact of Demographics on 21st Century Education. *Social Science and Public Policy 50*(3), 272–82. doi: 10.1007/s12115-013-9655-z.

Fayer, S., Lacey, A., and Watson, A. (2017). STEM Occupations: Past, Present, and Future. *Spotlight on Statistics*. Washington, DC: US Bureau of Labor Statistics. Retrieved from https://www.bls.gov.

Felton, E. (2018a). "It's like a black and white thing": How Some Elite Charter Schools Exclude Minorities. *The Hechinger Report*. June 17, 2018. Retrieved from https://

www.nbcnews/education/it-s-black-white-thing-how-some-elite-charter-schools-n878656.
Felton, E. (2018b). Nearly 750 Charter Schools Are Whiter Than the Nearby District Schools. *The Hechinger Report.* June 17, 2018. Retrieved from https://hechingerreport.org/nearly-750-charter-schools-are-whiter-than-the-nearby-district-schools.
Fisher, D., and Frey, N. (2008). *Better Learning through Structured Teaching: A Framework for the Gradual Release of Responsibility.* Alexandria, VA: Association for Supervision and Curriculum Development.
Fisher, D., and Frey, N. (2016). Designing Quality Content Area Instruction. *The Reading Teacher (69)*5, 525–29. doi: 10.1002/trtr.1446.
Fraser-Burgess, S. (2012). Group Identity, Deliberative Democracy, and Diversity in Education. *Educational Philosophy and Theory (44)*5, 480–501. doi: 10.1111/j.1469-5812.2010.00717.x.
Fullan, M. (1994). *Change Forces: Probing the Depths of Educational Reform.* Bristol, PA: Falmer Press.
Garcia, E., and Weiss, E. (2015). Early Education Gaps by Social Class and Race Start U.S. Children Out on Unequal Footing. *A Summary of the Major Findings in Inequalities at the Starting Gate.* Washington, DC: Economic Policy Institute. Retrieved from https://www.epi.org/publication/early-education-gaps-by-social-class-and-race-start-u-s-children-out-on-unequal-footing-a-summary-of-the-major-findings-in-inequalities-at-the-starting-gate/.
Garza, R. E., and Garza, Jr., E. (2010). Successful White Female Techers of Mexican American Students of Low Socioeconomic Status. *Journal of Latinos and Education (9)*3, 189–206. doi: 10.1080/15348431003761174.
Giroux, H. A. (2014). When Schools Become Dead Zones of the Imagination: A Critical Pedagogy Manifesto. *Policy Futures in Education (12)*4, 491–99. https://doi.org.10.2304/pfie.2014.12.4.491.
Goldstein, D. (2014). *The Teacher Wars: A History of America's Most Embattled Profession.* New York: Anchor Books.
Goodlad, J. (1984). *A Place Called School: Prospects for the Future.* New York: McGraw-Hill.
Goodson, I. (2007). All the Lonely People: The Struggle for Private Meaning and Public Purpose in Education. *Critical Studies in Education (48)*1, March 2007, 131–48. doi: 10.1080/17508480601120954.
Granger, D. A. (2008). No Child Left Behind and the Spectacle of Failing Schools: The Mythology of Contemporary School Reform. *Educational Studies 43*, 206–28. doi: 10.1080/00131940802117654.
Gunzenhauser, M. G. (2003). High-Stakes Testing and the Default Philosophy of Education. *Theory into Practice (42)*1, 51–59.
Hampton, F. M. (2016). The Seven Secrets of Successful Urban School Students: The Evidence Continues to Grow. *Education and Urban Society (48)*5, 423–43. doi: 10.1177/0013124514533990.
Harbour, K. E., Evanovich, L. L., Sweigart, C. A., and Hughes, L. E. (2015). A Brief Review of Effective Teaching Practices That Maximize Student Engagement. *Preventing School Failure 59*(1), 5–13. doi: 10.1080/1045988X.2014.919136.
Hart, Paul't. (1991). Irving L. Janis' Victims of Groupthink. *Political Psychology (12)*2, 247–78. Retrieved from http://www.jstor.org/stable/3791464.
Heafner, T. L., and Fitchett, P. C. (2015). An Opportunity to Learn US History: What NAEP Data Suggest Regarding the Opportunity Gap. *The High School Journal (98)*3, 226–49. doi: 10.1353/hsj.2015.0006.
Hefling, K. (2018a). Unraveling State Finances and Teacher Strikes. *POLITICO Morning Education.* May 15, 2018. Retrieved from https://www.politico.com/newsletters/morning-education/2018/05/15/unraveling-state-finances-and-teacher-strikes-218612.
Hefling, K. (2018b). K–12 Funding Battles Trigger Ballot Initiatives. *POLITICO Morning Education.* June 11, 2018. Retrieved from https://www.politico.com/newsletters/

morning-education/2018/06/11/k-12-funding-battles-trigger-ballot-initiatives-248155.

Hefling, K. (2018c). Opioid Epidemic Overwhelms Schools. *POLITICO Morning Education*. June 18, 2018. Retrieved from https://www.politico.com/newsletter/morning-education/2018/06/18/opioid-epidemic-overwhelms-schools-257387.

Honig, M. I., and Coburn, C. (2007). Evidence-Based Decision Making in School District Central Offices: Toward a Policy and Research Agenda. *Educational Policy (22)*4, 578–608. doi: 10.1177/0895904807307067.

Hunter, M. (2018). School Funding Litigation from Coast to Coast. *Education Law Center*. Retrieved from https://edlawcenter.org/news/archives/school-funding-national/school-funding-litigation-from-coast-to-coast.html.

IES/NCES (Institute for Education Sciences/National Center for Education Statistics). (2018). Characteristics of Children's Families. *The Condition of Education*. Washington, DC: US Department of Education. Retrieved from https://nces.ed.gov/programs/coe/indicator_cce.asp.

Ignelzi, M. (2000). Meaning-Making in the Learning and Teaching Process. *New Directions for Teaching and Learning 82*, 5–14. Summer 2000.

Ikpa, V. W. (2016). Politics, Adequacy, and Education. *Education (136)*4, 468–72.

Ilgen, D. R., Hollenbeck, J. R., Johnson, M., and Jundt, D. (2005). Teams in Organizations: From Input-Process-Output Models to IMOI Models. *Annual Review of Psychology 56*, 517–43. doi: 10.1146/annurev.psych.56.091103.070250.

Indiana Constitution. (1851). *Constitution of the State of Indiana Article 8, Section 1*. As amended 2016. Retrieved from www.law.indiana.edu; www.iga.in.gov.

Jacobsen, R., Snyder, J. W., and Saultz, A. (2014). Informing or Shaping Public Opinion? The Influence of School Accountability Data Format on Public Perceptions of School Quality. *American Journal of Education 121*, 1–25.

Jensen, J. L., McDaniel, M. A., Woodard, S. M., and Kummer, T. A. (2014). Teaching to the Test . . . or Testing to Teach: Exams Requiring Higher Order Thinking Skills Encourage Greater Conceptual Understanding. *Educational Psychology Review 26*, 307–29. doi: 10.1007/s10648-013-9248-9.

Knight Abowitz, K. (2011). Achieving Public Schools. *Educational Theory (61)*4, 467–89.

Kodrzycki, Y. K. (2002). Education in the 21st Century: Meeting the Challenges of a Changing World. *New England Economic Review*. Fourth Quarter 2002.

Kozol, J. (1991). *Savage Inequalities: Children in America's Schools*. New York: Crown Publishing.

Krathwohl, D. R. (2002). A Revision of Bloom's Taxonomy: An Overview. *Theory into Practice (41)*4, 212–18. Retrieved from https://www.depauw.edu/files/resources/krathwohl.

Lapsley, D. K. (2008). Moral Self-Identity and the Aim of Education. In Larry P. Nucci and Darcia Narvaez (Eds.), *Handbook of Moral and Character Education*, 30–50. New York: Routledge.

Lee, J., and Shute, V. J. (2010). Personal and Social-Contextual Factors in K–12 Academic Performance: An Integrative Perspective on Student Learning. *Educational Psychologist (45)*3, 185–202. doi: 10.1080/00461520.2010.493471.

Leonor, M. (2018). The Two-in-One Cabinet Agency. *POLITICO Morning Education*. June 22, 2018. Retrieved from https://www.politico.com/newsletters/morning-education/2018/06/22/the-two-in-one-cabinet-agency-261569.

Lubienski, C. (2013). Privatising Form or Function? Equity, Outcomes and Influence in American Charter Schools. *Oxford Review of Education (39)*4, 498–513. Retrieved from http://dx.doi.org/10.1080/03054985.2013.821853.

Malin, H. (2011). American Identity Development and Citizenship Education: A Summary of Perspectives and Call for New Research. *Applied Developmental Science (15)*2, 111–16. doi: 10.1080/10888691.2011.560817.

Marsh, J. A., and Wohlstetter, P. (2013). Recent Trends in Intergovernmental Relations: The Resurgence of Local Actors in Education Policy. *Educational Researcher (42)*5, 276–83. doi: 10.3102/0013189X13492193.

Matusov, E., and Smith, M. P. (2012). The Middle-Class Nature of Identity and Its Implications for Education: A Genealogical Analysis and Reevaluation of a Culturally and Historically Bounded Concept. *Integrative Psychological and Behavioral Science 46*, 274–95. doi: 10.1007/s12124-012-9192-0.

McMahon, T. R., Baete Kenyon, D., and Carter, J. S. (2013). "My Culture, My Family, My School, Me": Identifying Strengths and Challenges in the Lives and Communities of American Indian Youth. *Journal of Child and Family Studies 22*, 694–706. doi: 10.1007/s10826-012-9623-z.

McWilliam, E. (2008). Unlearning How to Teach. *Innovations in Education and Teaching International (45)*3, 263–69. doi: 10.1080/14703290802176147.

Mehta, S., and Finnegan, M. (2019). Segregation Has Soared in America's Schools as Federal Leaders Largely Looked Away. *Los Angeles Times*, July 8, 2019. Retrieved from https://www.latimes.com/la-na-pol-2020-school-segregation.

Mercer, N. (2013). The Social Brain, Language, and Goal-Directed Collective Thinking: A Social Conception of Cognition and Its Implications for Understanding How We Think, Teach, and Learn. *Educational Psychologist (48)*3, 148–68. Retrieved from https://doi.org/10.1080/00461520.2013.804394.

Mincu, M. E. (2015). Teacher Quality and School Improvement: What Is the Role of Research? *Oxford Review of Education (41)*2, 253–69. Retrieved from http://dx.doi.org/10.1080/03054985.2015.1023013.

Minkos, M. L., Sassu, K. A., Gregory, J. L., Patwa, S. S., Theodore, L. A., and Femc-Bagwell, M. (2017). Culturally Responsive Practice and the Role of School Administrators. *Psychology in the Schools (54)*10, 1260–66. Retrieved from https://doi.org/10.1002/pits.22072.

Molden, D. C., and Higgins, E. T. (2012). Motivated Thinking. In Keith J. Holyoak and Robert G. Morrison (Eds.), *The Oxford Handbook of Thinking and Reasoning*, 390–412. Retrieved from www.researchgate.net/publication313563127_Motivated_Thinking.

National Association of School Psychologists. (2014). Effective Parenting: Positive Support for Families. [*Position Statement*]. Bethesda, MD: Author.

NCES (National Center for Education Statistics). (2018). Public School Revenue Sources. *Preprimary, Elementary, and Secondary Education: Finances*. Retrieved from https://nces.ed.gov/programs/coe/pdf/coe_cma.pdf.

NPR (National Public Radio). (2018). America's Schools Are "Profoundly Unequal," Says US Civil Rights Commission. Retrieved from https://www.npr.org/sections/ed/2018/01/11/577000301/america's-schools-are-profoundly-unequal-says-u-s-civil-rights-commission.

Nucci, L. P. (2008). Social Cognitive Domain Theory and Moral Education. In Larry P. Nucci and Darcia Narvaez (Eds.), *Handbook of Moral and Character Education*, 291–309. New York: Routledge.

Ogbu, J. U. (2004). Collective Identity and the Burden of "Acting White" in Black History, Community, and Education. *The Urban Review (36)*1, 1–35.

Orfield, G., and Frankenberg, E. (2014). Increasingly Segregated and Unequal Schools as Courts Reverse Policy. *Educational Administration Quarterly (50)*5, 718–34. doi: 10.1177/0013161X4548942.

Palumbo, A., and Kramer-Vida, L. (2012). An Academic Curriculum Will Close the Academic Achievement Gap. *The Clearing House 85*(3), 117–21. doi: 10.1080/00098655.2012.655345.

Patrick, H., and Mantzicopoulos, P. (2016). Is Effective Teaching Stable? *The Journal of Experimental Education (84)*1, 23–47. doi: 10.1080/00220973.2014.952398.

PDK (Phi Delta Kappa). Retrieved from https://pdkpoll.org/assets/downloads/2019pdkpoll51.

Popham, W. J. (1999). Why Standardized Tests Don't Measure Educational Quality. *Educational Leadership (56)*6, March 1999.

Pritchett, L., and Viarengo, M. (2015). Does Public Sector Control Reduce Variance in School Quality? *Education Economics (23)*5, 557–76. Retrieved from http://dx.doi.org/10.1080/09645229.2015.1012152.

Reckhow, S., Grossman, M., and Evans, B. C. (2015). Policy Cures and Ideology in Attitudes toward Charter Schools. *Policy Studies Journal (43)*2. Retrieved from https://doi.org/10.1111/psj.12093.

Rector-Aranda, A. (2016). School Norms and Reforms, Critical Race Theory, and the Fairytale of Equitable Education. *Critical Questions in Education (7)*1, 1–16.

Reimers, F. (2006). Citizenship, Identity and Education: Examining the Public Purposes of Schools in an Age of Globalization. *Prospects (36)*3, 275–94.

Reisch, M. (2002). Defining Social Justice in a Socially Unjust World. *Families in Society: The Journal of Contemporary Human Services (83)*4, 343–54.

Roda, A., and Stuart Wells, A. (2013). School Choice Policies and Racial Segregation: Where White Parents' Good Intentions, Anxiety, and Privilege Collide. *Faculty Works: Education 46*. Retrieved from https://digitalcommons.molloy.edu/edu_fac.

Rodriguez, L. F. (2008). Latino School Dropout and Popular Culture: Envisioning Solutions to a Pervasive Problem. *Journal of Latinos and Education (7)*3, 258–64. doi: 10.1080/15348430802100402.

Roosevelt, E. (1937). *This Is My Story*. New York: HarperCollins.

Samel, A. N., Sondergeld, T. A., Fischer, J. M., and Patterson, N. C. (2011). The Secondary School Pipeline: Longitudinal Indicators of Resilience and Resistance in Urban Schools Under Reform. *The High School Journal (94)*3, 95–118. doi: 10.1353/hsj.2011.0005.

Shaffer, M. B., Ellis, J. G., and Swensson, J. (2018). Hoosier Lawmaker? Vouchers, ALEC Legislative Puppets, and Indiana's Abdication of Democracy. *AASA Journal of Scholarship and Practice (14)*4, 4–17.

Shapiro, E. (2018). How an Unknown Reformer Rescued One of America's Most Troubled School Districts. *POLITICO Magazine*, June 30, 2018. Retrieved from https://www.politico.com/magazine/story/2018/06/30/camden-superintendent-education-reform-paymon-rouhanifard-218940.

Shaw, J. S. (2010). Education—A Bad Public Good? *The Independent Review (15)*2, 241–56.

Sjoberg, S. (2012). PISA: Politics, Fundamental Problems and Intriguing Results. *La Revue, Recherches en Education 14*, 1–20.

Smith, R., and Lowery, L. (2017). Students Can't Wait: Promoting Equity and Improvement Through ESSA. *State Education Standard (17)*3, 7–10.

Snarey, J., and Samuelson, P. (2008). Moral Education in the Cognitive Development Tradition: Lawrence Kohlberg's Revolutionary Ideas. In Larry P. Nucci and Darcia Narvaez (Eds.), *Handbook of Moral and Character Education*, 53–80. New York: Routledge.

Stecher, Brian M. et al. (2018). Improving Teaching Effectiveness: Final Report, The Intensive Partnerships for Effective Teaching through 2015–2016. *RAND Corporation Final Report on Bill & Melinda Gates's "Intensive Partnerships for Effective Teaching" Initiative*. Retrieved from https://www.rand.org/pubs/research_RR2242.

Stein, M. L. (2015). Public School Choice and Racial Sorting: An Examination of Charter Schools in Indianapolis. *American Journal of Education 121*, 597–622.

Sternberg, R. J. (1997). A Triarchic View of Giftedness: Theory and Practice. In Nicholas Colangelo and Gary A Davis. (Eds.), *Handbook of Gifted Education*. Boston, MA: Allyn & Bacon.

Sternberg, R. J. (2002 December). Raising the Achievement of All Students: Teaching for Successful Intelligence. *Educational Psychology (14)*4, 383–93.

Sternberg, R. J. and Grigorenko, E. L. (2004 Autumn). Successful Intelligence in the Classroom. *Theory into Practice (43)*4, 274–80.

Stitzlein, S. M. (2015). Addressing Educational Accountability and Political Legitimacy with Citizen Responsibility. *Educational Theory (65)*5, 563–80.

Strike, K. A. (2008). School, Community and Moral Education. In Larry P. Nucci and Darcia Narvaez (Eds.), *Handbook of Moral and Character Education*, 117–33. New York: Routledge.

Swensson, J., and Ellis, J. (2016). Follow the Money: On the Road to Charters and Vouchers Via the Educational-Industrial Complex. *Journal of Educational Finance (41)*4, 391–418.

Swensson, J., Ellis, J., and Shaffer, M. (2019a). *Unraveling Reform Rhetoric: What Educators Need to Know and Understand.* Lanham, MD: Rowman & Littlefield.

Swensson, J., Ellis, J., and Shaffer, M. (2019b). *An Educator's GPS: Fending Off the Free Market of Schooling for America's Students.* Lanham, MD: Rowman & Littlefield.

Tichnor-Wagner, A., Harrison, C., and Cohen-Vogel, L. (2016). Cultures of Learning in Effective High Schools. *Educational Administration Quarterly (52)*4, 602–42. doi: 10.1177/0013161X16644957.

Umpstead, R. R. (2007). Determining Adequacy: How Courts Are Redefining State Responsibility for Educational Finance, Goals, and Accountability. *BYU Education and Law Journal* 2. Retrieved from https://digitalcommons.law.byu.edu/elj/vol2007/iss2/5.

US Commission on Civil Rights. (2018). Public Education Funding Inequity: In an Era of Increasing Poverty and Resegregation. *Briefing Report.* Washington, DC: US Commission on Civil Rights. Retrieved from https://www.usccr.gov/pubs/2018-01-10-Education-Inequity.

USDOE (United States Department of Education). (2018). School Statistics. *Fast Facts.* Retrieved from https://nces.ed.gov/fastfacts/display.asp?id=372.

Valenzuela, A. (2005). Subtractive Schooling, Caring Relations, and Social Capital in the Schooling of US-Mexican Youth. In L. Weis and M. Fine (Eds.), *Beyond Silenced Voices: Class, Race, and Gender in United States Schools.* Albany, NY: State University of New York Press.

Waldron, N. L., and McLeskey, J. (2010). Establishing a Collaborative School Culture through Comprehensive School Reform. *Journal of Educational and Psychological Consultation (20)*, 58–74. doi: 10.1080/10474410903535364.

Whitehurst, G. J. (2017). New Evidence on School Choice and Racially Segregated Schools. *Evidence Speaks Reports (33)*2. Retrieved from https://www.brookings.edu/wp-content/uploads/2017/12/whitehurst-report.

Wiggins, G., and McTighe, J. (2005). *Understanding by Design.* Alexandria, VA: Association for Supervision and Curriculum Development.

Worrell, F. C. (2014). Theories School Psychologists Should Know: Culture and Academic Achievement. *Psychology in the Schools (51)*4, 332–47. doi: 10.1002/pits.21756.

Index

21CPE. *See* Twenty-First-Century Comprehensive Public Education

accountability, 57, 61, 65, 119
adult-centric advantage, 10, 40, 41
agency, 22, 69, 76, 113, 136, 139
American Legislative Exchange Council (ALEC), 33, 59, 75, 104
a priori pedagogy, 85

Brown v. Board of Education , 16, 24

charter schools, 30, 99, 101
choice education, 15, 29, 60
collective identity, 78
common ground, 96, 107, 110, 112, 129, 136; intelligence of, 111
competition, 30, 31, 32, 36
conventional wisdom, 48, 51, 52

deficit thinking, 16, 43, 48, 56
democracy, 15, 24, 34, 38, 109, 110, 137, 138
double consciousness, 17
Du Bois, W. E. B., 17
dynamic instruction, 21, 68, 81, 84, 88, 92, 95, 116

education : constitutional provisions for, 14, 28, 35, 39, 49; contemporary purpose of, 1, 37, 70, 71, 98; funding for, 28, 51, 99, 127; moral obligation of, 15, 17, 24, 69, 117, 118, 121; original power of, 67, 68, 69, 70, 71, 72, 75, 127, 135; primary purpose of, 38, 73, 79, 116, 118, 121; traditional US public, 28, 32, 34, 126; US history and, 16, 23, 28, 109
educational adequacy, 4, 10, 38, 48, 49, 50, 51, 53, 118, 125, 133, 138, 142

educational function, 83, 84
enrollment, 4, 5, 68
evaluation: effective, 63, 64, 85, 105, 132; formative, 55; summative, 55

fog of certainty, 60, 61
free market: schooling, 15, 28, 29, 30, 31, 32, 72; theory, 5, 7
freedom, 76, 78, 139, 141
freedom vis-à-vis learning, 69, 77, 111, 139
funding: free market schools, 7, 33, 100; public schools, 6

gap-gazing, 61

habits of mind, 64, 94, 129; critical, 17, 20, 135, 141, 142; uncritical, 16, 70, 77, 78, 110
high school graduation, 6
how to think , 18, 36, 62, 67, 76, 79, 93, 94, 113

I identify as . . . statements, 76, 77, 122, 130
ideology, 33, 40, 41, 60, 73, 99, 100
instruction, 68, 83
instructional mapping, 85
instructional precursors, 86, 87
intentional self, 79, 142

knee-jerk pedagogy, 57, 61

languaging, 92, 93
learning, 68, 74, 90; styles, 82
linearity, 52, 53, 98; I-P-O model, 53, 55

measurement, 55, 57, 58, 59, 65, 104
mediational influence, 53, 123

No Child Left Behind (NCLB), 73, 102

pedagogical agency, 91
philosophy of education, 115, 117, 123, 134
policy, 97, 100, 101, 102, 103, 106; policy feedback theory, 106
positive liberty, 69
principled reasoning, 18, 19, 69, 76, 81, 135
privatization, 29, 32, 99
public good, 78, 108, 112, 140

racial opportunity cost, 17
reform, 3, 42, 101
Return on Investment (ROI), 44
Return to Students (RTS), 45, 83, 105
ROI. *See* Return on Investment
RTS. *See* Return to Students

school-attached, 43
school-detached, 43, 48
self-mastery, 19
singularity, 15, 30, 31, 42, 78, 98
social contract, 23, 40, 78, 111, 112, 137
social justice, 20, 23, 137, 140, 142

standardized testing, 8, 55, 56, 57, 131
stereotype threat, 77
students, 4, 5, 10, 16, 21, 22, 38, 44, 50, 107, 122, 126, 138; engagement of, 89, 90, 92, 94
subordination, 78
successful intelligence, 9
synergy of struggle, 39, 45, 70

teaching, 21, 68
TEO. *See* Tyranny of either/or
test prep, 57, 62
the functionally public school, 120
the good, 18, 20, 22, 138
the good public school, 2, 11, 120, 123, 137, 141
throughput, 53
True North, 13, 24, 119
Twenty-First-Century Comprehensive Public Education (21CPE), 11, 25, 74, 79, 108, 118, 123, 125, 140
Tyranny of either/or (TEO), 39, 40, 41, 42, 44

workforce development, 71, 98

About the Authors

Jeff Swensson served in traditional public education as a teacher, assistant principal, principal, assistant superintendent, and superintendent across the Midwest for the past forty-five years. He graduated from Amherst College, received his MAT from Northwestern University, and earned his PhD from Indiana University.

Michael Shaffer served in schools in Kentucky, Pennsylvania, Indiana, and Iowa as an assistant principal, principal, and assistant superintendent. He graduated from Morehead State University with a BA and MA in elementary education and earned his Education Specialist and Education Doctorate in Educational Leadership from Ball State University.

www.ingramcontent.com/pod-product-compliance
Lightning Source LLC
Chambersburg PA
CBHW020333240426
43665CB00043B/511